Fish, Oil, & Follies

Fish Wars and Oil Battles of an Alaska Biologist and Fishing Guide

Loren B. Flagg

PO Box 221974 Anchorage, Alaska 99522-1974
books@publicationconsultants.com—www.publicationconsultants.com

ISBN 978-1-59433-094-0
Library of Congress Catalog Card Number: 2009923854

Cover art by Jim Evensen. Cover design by Brian Parker

Manufactured in the United States of America.

Acknowledgements

First and foremost I thank my wife Sandra who provided the inspiration to get this project started. Upon seeing boredom set in during my first winter of full retirement she asked, "Dear, why don't you write a book?" Sandra also deserves credit for providing most of the photos appearing in this book and for editorial assistance.

Once I started composing on the computer I immediately needed help in formatting and other vagaries of word processing. Who else to help but a teenage grandson? Thank you Lee Benson Kempf.

When I sent in an early sample chapter from my manuscript to my publisher, Evan Swensen, he immediately saw I was going to need professional editorial assistance. Thanks to Marthy Johnson in Anchorage for providing this help.

As the project progressed I sent out chapters to a few of my friends for review and comment. Jim Rearden provided much needed encouragement and an overview of how to proceed in getting a book from rough draft to final product. Tom Kizzia reviewed several of the chapters on Homer and Kachemak Bay and made many helpful suggestions. Frank Tupper provided review and needed support on the Kachemak Bay oil lease chapter. Carl Divinyi and David Albury helped refresh my memory of events we shared while working in the Florida Everglades. Gary Williams provided encouragement, corrections, and helpful comments. Connie Gatling gave much needed help with punctuation.

My sister, Susan Flagg Poole, spent many hours reading through the entire manuscript and provided corrections and editorial comments throughout. Susan suggested several changes in chapter headings, integration, organization and helped greatly with the overall flow of the book. My sister-in-law, Donna Flagg, reviewed the final proof and made some spelling corrections, and also helped clarify some of the finer points of the English language. Loren Leman also reviewed the final proof and made some helpful comments and corrections

Finally, I thank my publisher, Evan Swensen, for helping me from the very beginning with encouragement, suggestions, and expert advice in navigating the sometimes rocky road between an idea, a draft, and the actual completion of a book.

Contents

Foreword
by Jim Rearden

Loren Flagg, author of this book, has two passions; he loves to catch fish, and he is a dedicated conservationist (believes in wise use of fish and wildlife). Readers of his book will quickly learn that his working life has been spent mostly conserving fish, and that he has also spent much of his spare time catching them with rod and reel.

In this nicely written personal history, Loren generously shares much information on where and how to catch fish in Alaska and elsewhere—and he has included many photos to prove his ability as a rod and reel fisherman, and a fishing guide.

In 1968 I was the Area Biologist for commercial fisheries in Cook Inlet for the Alaska Department of Fish and Game, stationed at Homer, and I needed another assistant. I looked for a hands-on scientifically-trained field guy, who would be willing to get fish slime on his hands, and who wouldn't be nervous in small planes and aboard small boats at sea.

I hired Loren, even though most of his fisheries experience was in Florida. Strangely, there were trained fisheries biologists in western and northern states, but few seemed interested in moving to Alaska. Flagg made it clear he was eager to move North. He was born and raised in New England, where the climate and many conditions are similar to those of coastal Alaska, so the change wasn't that great for him. His resume was well done, and he made it clear that he preferred field work, not desk work. While working for me, he got his wish; he was often wet, muddy, and covered with fish slime, and he spent a lot of time on boats at sea, and insmall planes. Some people are meant to become Alaskans, and Loren Flagg is one of them. Eventually, he even took over my job as Area Biologist, although he didn't want it, which makes an interesting story which he recounts herein. In this year of 2009, Loren and his wife Sandra are still Alaskans after moving here forty-one years ago, and I have no doubt they will remain so.

While working in and around Kachemak Bay, one of the world's most beautiful, and at the same time one of the most productive anywhere, Loren became an authority on the bay. He knew what it produced, how its waters moved, and its fisheries history. His reports (he did ok at desk work, as well as at field work) made clear that this bay is special.

When, in December, 1973, Alaska's Department of Natural Resources, which leases lands for oil and mineral production, rushed through an oil lease sale for Kachemak Bay, they didn't bother to hold a public hearing. The lease was to be squarely on the most important crab breeding grounds. At the time, commercial fishermen annually landed about one and a half million pounds of king crab from Kachemak Bay.

The White Knight who galloped front and center to play a key role in reversing the sale was Loren Flagg. His data, knowledge, backbone, ability, and dedication saved lovely Kachemak Bay from sprouting ugly oil rigs, and perhaps oil spills. His recounting of this event is as dramatic a scenario on politics and conservation as one can find anywhere.

Loren's experience with the Kachemak Bay oil lease program of the DNR put him in direct line of action for the protection of Cook Inlet during the 1989 mammoth Exxon Valdez oil spill. Kenai Peninsula Borough Mayor Don Gilman named him chairman of the Multi-Agency Coordination Advisory Council that was established to attempt to cope with the Exxon oil that washed the outer Kenai Peninsula and into Cook Inlet. He has become a recognized expert on oil spills and their prevention.

Since his retirement from the Department of Fish and Game, whenever mismanagement of the Cook Inlet salmon fishery has taken place, whether through politics, ignorance, or greed, Loren has made his voice heard. He has been involved with numerous organizations aimed at conservation (wise use) of the Cook Inlet salmon fishery. Although he is retired as a fishery biologist, and retired from twenty years as a fishing guide, he isn't retired when it comes to a fight to see that the fishery is properly managed. It's all here.

The kid with Florida fisheries experience I hired as my assistant all those years ago has done all right.

Introduction

These things I saw and some of them I was.
Virgil

I grew up on a hill just above the banks of the Elmwood River in southeastern Massachusetts. Above Elmwood, this waterway was known as the Matfield River; below—after it joined the Satuckut River and flowed through the town of Bridgewater—the river became the Taunton. The Taunton River played a large role in the early days of the Pilgrims and their trading with the Wampanoag Indians, whose tribal leader Massasoit lived near the river mouth. Massasoit, his son King Philip, Plymouth Colony Governor's Edward Windslow and William Bradford—all traveled up and down the Taunton River on their trading trips throughout the early Pilgrim days.

I loved the Elmwood River and spent my early years hunting, fishing, and trapping along the river and its tributaries. These early experiences led to a wildlife and fisheries management major at the University of Massachusetts (UMASS) in Amherst. While at UMASS, the Connecticut River was just twenty minutes and a few casts away. After graduation the Massachusetts Division of Inland Fisheries hired me in a temporary position as a fisheries biologist. I got to travel around the state taking inventory and sampling fish populations in many rivers and lakes. The day President Kennedy was shot I was pulling up fish traps on Thoreau's Walden Pond in Concord. One week later I was on my way to Florida with my wife, Sandra, and two kids, Laurie and Mitch.

I had been hired by the Florida Game and Fresh Water Fish Commission as a fisheries biologist and had been assigned to a research project in the Florida Everglades. For the next three and one half years I was stationed in Fort Lauderdale and traveled from there to work in the "glades" an average of three to four days per week. The Everglades Conservation Area is where I got my next fisheries experience—cruising by airboat, sampling, and fishing a huge area south of Lake Okeechobee, known as "The River of Grass."

The project wound down about the same time I tired of the excessive heat and humidity. Applications went out to Massachusetts and Alaska. The Massachusetts Division of Marine Fisheries responded first and in June 1967, we were on our way to New England. I was hired as a marine biologist and stationed at Shawme-Crowell State Forest in Sandwich. Here I had my first opportunity to get my feet wet in marine fisheries. We worked up and down Cape Cod assisting local shellfish wardens on evaluation and enhancement projects. I also got my first taste of oil spill damage assessment following a bunker oil spill that wiped out most of the marine life at a small lagoon near Falmouth.

After six months on this project Alaska beckoned. I received a telegram from the Alaska Department of Fish and Game (ADF&G) offering me a position as a Fisheries Biologist ll. The starting salary was exactly double what I was presently making, although that really wasn't the main factor in my decision. I had wanted to go to Alaska since I was a freshman in high school and I actually would have taken less money! I had to pick between a job in Homer and one in Anchorage. In early February 1968, I loaded everything we owned into a Dodge Sportsvan and with my dad as companion headed up the Alaska Highway bound for Homer. For the next eleven and one-half years I worked in salmon management, shellfish management, oil pollution response, and marine research in Kachemak Bay and Lower Cook Inlet. I ended up playing a key role in the Kachemak Bay oil lease controversy, which raged on from 1973-1977. When not working for ADF&G, I spent quite a bit of time sport fishing around Kachemak Bay and on the nearby Anchor River.

After the Kachemak Bay research project was completed I took a job with ADF&G up the road about seventy miles in Soldotna. I was involved in assessing the results of various fisheries enhancement projects that had recently been started within and along tributaries of the Kenai and Kasilof rivers. I spent significant field time on these rivers, both as a fisheries research biologist and as a sports fisherman. Living on the Kenai River in Soldotna I, of course, had to have a riverboat. When the ADF&G bosses, or dignitaries from other state or federal agencies came to town I was the guy assigned to "show them" the Kenai River. Since "show them" also meant, "*let's go fishing*," this eventually led to a guide career.

In 1987 I took advantage of the first "early retirement" program offered by the State of Alaska and shortly thereafter applied for my Kenai River guide license. With all the contacts I had developed within the various state and federal resource agencies I had a great client base and no problem getting off to a good start in my new business. Shortly after my retirement from the state I also worked as a consultant for the Cook Inlet commercial fishing industry. During this period I was hired by the Kenai Peninsula Borough to head up the Cook Inlet area response to the *Exxon Valdez* oil spill.

Now, after twenty years of guiding on the "world-famous" Kenai River, I have hung it up. This book highlights some of the experiences I have had along the paths between my boyhood on the Elmwood River and my retirement as a sport-fishing guide on the Kenai River. The main theme is my experience in various fisheries—sport and commercial—and the interaction I have played a part in between the fishing and oil industries in Alaska.

Chapter 1
Uncle Charlie the Fish Tutor

My uncle, Charlie Benson, had just returned from serving with the Army Rangers during World War II. He had served in Africa, Italy, and in the summer of 1944 found himself in southern France shortly after the Normandy invasion. He was honorably discharged following the war and when the summer of 1947 rolled around he must have been looking for a partner to share his favorite pastime—sport fishing. I was six years old and evidently available. Maybe he was just trying to help my mom out with babysitting duty, but I'd like to think he found me an enthusiastic fishing partner. Whatever the reason, I became Uncle Charlie's sidekick on untold numbers of fishing expeditions over the next few years.

I don't remember the very first outing, probably because it ended with my landing hard on my head on the side of the road. Charlie related the story to me a year before he died. He had taken me to a small pond located on the Bridgewater State Farm, a maximum security prison that would two decades later be home to one Albert DeSalvo, better know as the Boston Strangler. We had traveled that day in my Dad's 1933 Chevrolet panel truck which was our would-be means of transportation to many fishing sites in the years to come. There were no seat belts back then and the rickety old truck had doors that would often swing open with just a little bit of jarring. We had finished fishing for bass and bluegills and were on a bumpy dirt road leading out to the paved road when Charlie rounded a corner and, unbeknown to him at the time, lost his passenger! He had evidently been distracted watching the convicts working in the farm fields and was oblivious to the fate of his young fishing buddy. When Charlie hit the paved road that led back to the town of

Bridgewater he looked to the right to check for traffic. It was at that moment he realized that little Loren was missing.

When Uncle Charlie told me the story years later he said that at no time in his life, including his experiences in WW II, had he felt such raw fear. He turned the truck back onto the dirt road and drove back about a half mile, where he found me sitting by the side of the road, dazed but otherwise OK. I don't think he ever told my mom and dad or otherwise I might not have gone along on subsequent fishing trips. Since I never heard this story until the last year of Charlie's life, I guess it was sort of a near deathbed confession!

Over the next few years Uncle Charlie and I explored dozens of lakes, ponds, and rivers in the Plymouth County area of southeastern Massachusetts. We fished for bass, bluegills, sunfish, yellow perch, horned pout, and chain pickerel around the towns of Bridgewater, Halifax, Carver, Middleboro, and Pembroke. He taught me how to catch nightcrawlers by flashlight, how to tie fish line knots, bait hooks, and cast a level wind reel. Most of all, I guess he lighted a fishing flame within me that is still burning nearly six decades later.

Chapter 2
Elmwood: A River Runs Through It

Elmwood is a very small town in southeastern Massachusetts about midway between Boston and Cape Cod. The Elmwood post office was established by President Abraham Lincoln during the Civil War for the purpose of shipping shoes to Union troops. This post office is still in its original building nearly 150 years later and as such holds the distinction of being the oldest post office building in continuous use in the United States. My family owned this building and ran the post office for more than 100 years, starting with my great-grandfather Loren Augustus Flagg in 1898, and ending with the retirement of my sister, Sally Aldrich, as Elmwood postmaster in 2004.

The house I grew up in was an old New England colonial house that was in the Flagg family for ninety eight years. It sat on a hill just above the Elmwood River. This river was my backyard and playground for the first eighteen years of my life. A short walk out back and I was in my boat—ready to hunt, fish, trap, or just explore.

During my childhood, the Elmwood River was badly polluted by the city of Brockton's dysfunctional sewage treatment system. Although I caught a lot of fish from this river, I never ate one. A short way downstream from our house, the Elmwood River was joined by the Satucket, a much cleaner river that had a more healthy and robust fish population. In my teens I caught largemouth bass up to six pounds from the confluence of the two rivers.

King of the River

The Elmwood River was full of muskrats during the 1950s and I learned to trap them at an early age. One of my early role models was an elderly gentleman named Percy Stetson. Percy taught me a great deal about the ways of the river, about trapping, hunting, fishing and sporting ethics. Percy held the title of "King of the Elmwood River" during the late '40s and early '50s. He had earned the title by consistently trapping the most muskrats from the river. Percy had to slow down following a heart attack in 1954 and the title went to an infamous Elmwood bachelor and woodsman, Winnie Sherman. I never thought that I could upstage the more experienced Winnie, but thanks to expert tutelage from Percy and a thorough reading of *Fur Fish & Game* magazine, I eventually gained the knowledge and experience to take over the title. The year was 1956 and as a sophomore in high school I caught 82 muskrats and surpassed Winnie by a wide margin.

About a mile up the Satucket River from the confluence with the Elmwood was the Carver Cotton Ginworks. A small dam had been built above the Ginworks to provide hydroelectric power to the plant. This dam backed up the Satucket River and created the Ginworks pond. This pond became my favorite fishing hole since it was just a short bike ride away. The pond produced sunfish, yellow perch, largemouth bass, and horned pout. It was a great backup plan during times when Uncle Charlie was away on a construction job in Greenland and Mom or Dad were not available. At the upper part of the Ginworks pond were the remnants of an old Wampanoag Indian fish weir, constructed of large stones. Adjacent to the Ginworks on the southeast side was Sachem Rock, where in 1649 the Indians, represented by Massasoit, had traded away their land rights in the Bridgewaters area to the Pilgrims, represented by Myles Standish.

There were several other small ponds within bicycle range of Elmwood. So when adult transportation was not available, Plan B would go into effect. My childhood buddies Ronnie Thrasher, David Whitman, and John Campbell (Beanie) were almost always ready for a fishing adventure on a moment's notice. Or my cousin Brad Hall rode his bike down from Brockton and we would be off down the Elmwood River or to other nearby fishing holes. It was amazing what you could do in those days with no (or lousy) TV and no computers or other gadgets to play games on! We spent our time outdoors and mostly with little or no adult supervision. And I'm talking about starting at age seven or eight! If we weren't off fishing or hunting with our BB guns, we were off playing baseball, football, basketball, or hockey. Often as not these activities were not organized or supervised by adults but solely by a few of us kids in our pre-or early teens. We would organize competitions with kid's teams in adjoining towns and sometimes travel five or more miles away in sort of a team "bike brigade" to the game site. Looking back now, we seemed to operate pretty independently, much like Charlie Brown and his Peanuts gang.

Elmwood to the Cape

Cousin Brad and the Hall family had a summer cottage on Buttermilk Bay near the entrance to the Cape Cod Canal. I was fortunate to spend a part of each summer at the cottage, where Brad and I had access to an old wooden dory. When we were pre-teens we would row around Buttermilk Bay fishing for flounders and catching blue crab with a net and sometimes with our bare hands. Once we were in our teens we were allowed to use a 10-horsepower Johnson motor and now we had access to the canal where we usually targeted fluke but occasionally strippers and blues. There was a small lake within walking distance of the cottage that had some good-sized pickerel. This lake was heavily bordered with lily pads so the fishing technique from shore was to cast beyond the lily pads, retrieve the daredevil to the edge of the pads, and if by then there was no strike—jerk the lure up and over the pads landing it back along the shoreline. Needless to say this was risky business and sure enough I got my first serious hook injury trying to catch a stupid pickerel. Maybe the sun was in my eyes but on one retrieve I failed to duck and drove two of the three treble hooks completely through my upper lip. A quick trip to the doctor in Bourne and Brad and I were back chasing crab that evening!

My Dad, who never took fishing too seriously, did like to fish the Cape Cod Canal. For some reason it always seemed to be in the middle of the night and for some other reason I don't think we ever caught anything. I remember wading out a ways and casting wooden top water plugs as far upstream into the current as we could in hopes (dreams actually) of catching striped bass. Once we got tired of casting, Dad built a small fire alongside the canal and as brother Dave and I downed our hot chocolates, Dad would sip away on his blackberry brandy. These trips would usually end up with an early morning breakfast stop at A.R. Parker's restaurant in East Bridgewater, where Uncle Charlie worked, and tall tales were often heard!

Expeditions North

Other expeditions during this time of my life included annual summer trips north to White Lake in New Hampshire where the family camped out in a wall tent for one or two weeks. We used the old 1933 Chevy panel truck to haul our gear up there and that was always an adventure in itself! At White Lake, when we were not swimming, hiking, or working around camp, I had the opportunity to flail away from shore for trout. Occasionally, brother David and I borrowed or rented a boat for more serious attempts at fishing the lake or just to explore around. On the return trip from White Lake we always stopped at Lake Winnipesaukee to visit friends of my folks, who had a cottage there. Stopping for a day or two at this lake provided me with another chance to work on my fishing skills.

Expeditions South

During the early 1950s the family made a couple automobile trips down south to Winter Park, Florida, where my Uncle Jimmy and Aunt Ruth had built a home on the shores of Killarney Lake. This is where I caught my first Florida largemouth bass and had my first alligator encounter. Jimmy had an old 16-wheeler truck inner tube that I would float around on—one hand on a paddle, the other on a fishing pole. One time the wind came up and blew me across to the far side of the lake. There was pandemonium on shore, where Uncle Jimmy and my Dad were trying to locate a boat for the rescue as the women scurried about and screamed across the lake toward me. Jimmy, operating the outboard motor on a borrowed boat, sheared a pin taking off from the landing. By the time this problem was fixed and they were ready for a second try at rescue, I had calmly paddled back to safety. To add to the adventure, a large alligator that had been sunning itself on an adjacent lot quietly slid into the lake and headed out in my direction as I was paddling back toward shore. It must have presented quite a contrast—the panic and shrill screams coming from the safety of shore—to the relaxed and oblivious smile on my face as I returned undaunted by the excitement of the moment.

Chapter 3
Changing Streams

Life in many ways began to change when I turned sixteen and got my first driver's license. The good fishing holes were now more within reach for I had access to the old Chevy panel truck. I like to think that the fish were also significantly more endangered! Later I had my first car, a 1947 black Ford sedan to pursue fish, and now of course another quarry—girls! Sometimes I was lucky enough to have both. In my mid-teens I met my future wife, Sandra Kelley, and she was often game to accompany me on late-night fishing trips to the banks of the Cape Cod Canal and on other fishing safaris.

My best friend in my teen years was Ned Handy, known among his athlete friends as "Moose" for his size. Ned and I fished together, hunted together, and double-dated when the bass weren't biting. We both married our high-school sweethearts and remain best friends today. After graduation from high school Ned went off to Boston University on a football scholarship while I entered UMASS on a combined football/track scholarship. Both married entering college, we juggled our time between our families (each eventually with two kids), studies, and sports. During the summers we worked as truck drivers for a beverage company, Simpson Springs.

Ned and I loved to fish bass at night and after work we ventured out to some of the best known bass ponds in Plymouth County. Back then we used a weedless frog imitation which had been developed by a Baystate bass guru named Bill Plummer. We worked along shallow lily-padded shorelines and lived for the moment we would see a wake plowing toward our little fake frogs. I didn't keep a fish log back then, but I do recall we took a good number of bass in the four to six pound range. These were good sized bass for Massachusetts but we knew that other fishermen had taken fish in the eight to nine pound range, and that was always our goal. Once we both saw a giant of a bass moving through the weeds while night-fishing in Robbin's Pond. We both thought this fish was twice as big as anything we'd ever caught and that kept us coming back for some time after.

At UMASS I majored in physical education during my first year but didn't enjoy the total jock atmosphere that seemed to prevail in the P.E. department at the time. When I related this to Ned during the next summer he encouraged me to switch to a major in wildlife or fisheries, as he thought that would be a natural for me. I soon made the switch to a major in wildlife and fisheries biology. This was one of the major "Robert Frost" moments in my life where "*two roads diverged in a wood ...*" I'm not sure that I took the one less traveled but surely I changed course, and that has made all the difference.

From UMASS the Connecticut River was a short drive to the west; the Quabbin Reservoir a short drive east. These were two of my favorite fishing holes during the next four years. My buddies and I fished the Connecticut at night for bullheads and channel catfish and the Quabbin during daytime for trout—lakers, rainbows, browns, and brookies. There was also a small mill pond about a mile north of campus that I could escape to for a quick fishing trip when the combined stress of keeping up with studies and fulfilling the obligations of an athletic scholarship got to me.

Frozen Fish Lives!

My buddy and classmate Eddie Scrocki introduced me to ice fishing while at UMASS. We would drive up to Lake Champlain and set up a small shack about a half mile out on the ice a few miles south of Burlington, Vermont. Eddie knew where the big northern pike hung out and we had pretty good success catching fish through the ice in the 5-to-10 pound range. On one trip, the weather was miserable with the temperature in the minus teens and the wind blowing a near gale. When a flag went up we ran out of the shack (where we kept warm with brandy and a small Coleman stove), quickly pulled-up the pike, rebaited, and then ran back in full retreat mode. We noticed that the pike instantly froze as they were pulled out of the water. We threw five or six nice-sized pike into the car trunk and made the three or four hour drive back down to UMASS. We unloaded the pike, which were still frozen up like cordwood, into my kitchen sink and ran some water over them to start thawing them out. They had been frozen stiff for more than five hours but damned if they didn't start trying to swim around the sink when they thawed out! I related this to my fisheries professor and I got a great biology lesson. Certain fish species, pike included, actually have an antifreeze protein in their blood that allows them to survive below freezing conditions.

First Job

I got another great lesson, although not in biology, late in my senior year. This is a great lesson for anyone applying for a job. A job recruiter for the Massachusetts Division of Inland Fisheries had come to campus looking for a wildlife/fisheries major to fill a fisheries technician job in Westboro. There were two of us grads who were interested. One was a straight-A student who was to graduate at the top of his class. I was the other and had struggled all four years trying to maintain passing grades while fulfilling the dual obligations of athletic scholarship demands and raising a family that had now grown to four. In my major courses I had managed all A's and B's; however, all other required courses had dragged me down to just an average student. I didn't think I had much of a chance against the class valedictorian! We were told by the recruiter to submit an application with a letter of interest and transcript of grades. I put my main effort into the letter of interest and then started applying for other jobs. Lo and behold, I got hired for the fisheries technician job! After a short time on the job I asked my boss why I got hired over the smartest kid on campus. He said it was because I had applied in a more professional manner with a well-thought-out and neatly typed letter of interest. The other guy had just scribbled a few lines on note paper, probably thinking his outstanding grades would make him a shoo-in. I was to apply this valuable lesson several times in future career job pursuits.

Chapter 4
Fish Killer on the Loose

I spent the next six months with the Massachusetts Division of Inland Fisheries sampling and killing freshwater fish. Lots of fish! I quickly learned that killing fish, or renovating lakes as they called it, was a big part of this job during the summer and fall of 1963. When fish populations get out of balance, with perhaps too many bluegills or perch, and not enough bass—a chemical called rotenone was used to kill off all the fish in a lake. After the lake detoxified, it was then stocked with an appropriate ratio of desired fish species. We put out several thousand gallons of rotenone that summer and fall in lakes ranging from the Berkshires in western Massachusetts to way out on Cape Cod to the east. At times, it would appear that killing off some of these lakes was unwarranted, since 5-to-6 pound largemouth bass or trout up to 10-pounds would surface gasping for air after the rotenone was applied. As a temporary fisheries technician, who was I to question decisions regarding state fisheries management? Actually, I believe that the vast majority of the lake renovations that summer were well justified with tens of thousands of stunted sunfish or yellow perch often eliminated from these lakes in order to allow for the introduction of more desirable fish populations.

In addition to renovating lakes, we also conducted fish sampling all across the state. This would either involve netting or the use of an electric "fish shocker" to stun fish to the surface in order to sample them for age, weight, and length (AWL). A generator was mounted on the bow of the boat and attached to two electrodes, which extended down several feet into the water. The "juice" was controlled by a foot pedal also mounted in the bow. As the boat cruised the shoreline, the fisheries technician hit the pedal, sending a charge of electricity down into the water. Any fish in the vicinity was stunned and then floated up to the surface, where they could be netted for sampling. Most often these fish would recover and could then be released after the biological information was obtained.

I was one lucky guy to have this job! During the week I was in a position, through a paid job, to locate all the big-bass hot spots around the state. Often this work took me to the very southeastern Massachusetts lakes and ponds that my buddy Ned Handy and I had been fishing the last few years. Well, guess what Ned and I then did on weekends?! Yeah, this probably wasn't fair, but it sure was productive!

What about Bob?

One of the senior fisheries biologists working out of Westboro at the time we'll call Bob. He was an excellent biologist, but also the epitome of the absent minded professor. Bob kept us all in stitches with his antics. This was Bob in action:

1. Bob had been working by himself on a lake renovation project twenty five miles from the Westboro headquarters. At the end of the day he loaded his work boat onto the boat trailer and headed back to the shop. A half hour later he pulled into the parking area at the shop and made a wide swing to get aligned for backing the boat into the designated parking space. It was at this point that he became aware of a small problem—there was no boat to be backed up! Bob quickly retraced his route all the way back to the lake. There was the boat—100 yards from the lake alongside the railroad tracks where he had unknowingly dumped it. He didn't have a clue that he had lost it over the bumpy tracks less than a minute from the lake!

2. Bob was in the bow and controlling the foot pedal on the state electric shocking boat. He leaned over to net a fish and fell in face first. Somehow the foot pedal got stuck in the on-position and Bob was stunned just like a big largemouth bass. As the story goes, he was in a sort of semiconscious state when the propeller of the boat raked across his back. The boat operator—not me, thank God—circled back and fished Bob out of the water. Several stitches and liberal amounts of burn medicine were later applied. Bob never was allowed to run the shocker boat again.

3. Bob was doing a creel survey along the east side of the Connecticut River. He had pulled into a parking area that was on a downslope about 200 feet above the riverbank. He grabbed his clipboard, measuring tape and scale and started walking downhill to interview a group of fishermen below on the bank of the river. Bob was about half way down to the edge of the river when his truck nearly ran him over on its downhill journey to the bottom of the Connecticut River. Bob had forgot to set his parking brake! When the truck was later pulled out there was a 6-pound catfish swimming around the floor of the cab. Bob had a bad day, but he did eat well that evening!

4. I was part of a group of fishery technicians and biologists who were tagging fish from a raceway at one of the fish hatcheries near Westboro. There were several hundred trout to tag and this was going to be an all-day project. We had started out joking around a bit but as the work grew more tedious a long period of silence had fallen over the work party. The silence was broken by a loud splash just behind us. Bob had gone into one of his fogs, forgotten where he was, and taken a couple steps backwards falling into the raceway. As he flailed away in about 4 feet of water, trout went flying in all directions. We pulled him out and to his credit he went right back to the job at hand without even bothering to change his clothes. About an hour later one of the biologists noticed a dead trout sticking out from Bob's back pocket!

5. Several of us were working picking up dead fish following a lake renovation project. Bob and I were running the two work boats, ferrying workers to various locations around the lake. Bob took off across the lake by himself and was in the middle of the lake when I heard his 20 hp Merc outboard racing in an unusual way. Looking across the lake, I spotted Bob in the water and his boat racing at full speed and doing concentric circles around him. He had let go of the tiller to pull up his boots and the result was not what he had expected. The boat, as it circled, was moving in the direction of the wind down the lake and rapidly closing in on a helpless Bob. I remembered the scars along his back from the shocker boat incident and was thinking like Yogi Berra—*Deja` vu all over again.* I headed out to Bob in the other work boat and by the time I reached him, his boat, circling like a shark, was on its final approach. There was only

one thing to do—ram and sink the circling boat. As I rammed and rode up over the boat it changed course and ended up sinking about 10 feet off to the side of Bob. He swam to my boat, climbed aboard, thanked me, and went about working the rest of the day as if nothing had happened. That was Bob!

JFK and Walden Pond

The final project I worked on for the Massachusetts Division of Fisheries was the renovation of Walden Pond. This was the pond where Henry David Thoreau built a small cabin, spent a year and, of course, wrote a book about his experience. We had rotenoned the lake in mid-November and I had returned on November 20 to set test cages out to see if the lake had detoxified. I returned again on November 22 to check the cages to see if fish had survived. They had not, so we were going to need a few more days before the pond could be restocked. It was a nice day and some people were actually driving around with their windows down. When I stopped at a red light to make a left turn onto Route 9 I overheard the radio in a car that had pulled up alongside me: *Three shots were fired at President Kennedy's motorcade today in downtown Dallas, Texas.* When I got back to the shop in Westboro I heard the rest of the story.

Chapter 5
River of Grass

One week after President Kennedy was shot I loaded the family and everything we owned into our Plymouth station wagon and headed south to Florida. I had been hired by the Florida Game and Freshwater Fish Commission as a Fisheries Biologist 1 and was to be stationed in Ft. Lauderdale. I was to sample (i.e., kill) a lot more fish in my new position for the next three and one half years for the sake of science. My assignment was to a Federal Aid research project designed to assess the effects of ditching and diking on fisheries populations in the Florida Everglades Conservation Areas. Marjory Stoneham Douglas referred to the Everglades as the *River of Grass* in her book

The author, at age 24, displays a 9 3/4 pound Florida largemouth bass he caught fishing in the Everglades Conservation Area.

by that name in 1947. My new boss was Walt Dineen, an excellent fisheries biologist who in time became one of the foremost experts on the ecology of the Florida Everglades.

Fisheries Research.

We employed several sampling techniques to assess fish populations in the Everglades, but by far the most effective, and thus most commonly used, was rotenone. First we laid out a "block net," which was more than 800 feet long and when laid out in a square pattern covered exactly one square acre. The Conservation Areas were huge, more than one million acres, and thus required a large sample size to adequately assess fish populations. Next we applied the required amount of rotenone to obtain a total fish kill within the enclosed area. Barrels of rotenone were carried in our airboat and applied utilizing a pump and hose. After the chemical was applied we left the site for an hour or two and went off to fish for largemouth bass. Returning to the site we would circle with the airboat and pick up as many eating size fish as possible while they were still in good condition. Since rotenone affected only the gills of the fish through suffocation, fish killed by this method were still good to eat when captured shortly after the application.

Many poor families were living in rural areas between the Everglades and the Fort Lauderdale to Miami area. Both white and black folks lived at the level of poverty where you are always wondering where your next meal is coming from. That is where the fish from our day of sampling would end up—on the dinner tables of these folks. Walt and I didn't feel quite so bad about killing all these fish after we made our afternoon deliveries.

For the next two days we returned to the sample site and picked up every dead fish, regardless of size or species. Every fish was weighed and measured—a tedious task to say the least. After we had picked up what we could from the airboat, we then got out and waded around the sample area picking up remaining fish lodged in the sawgrass or under lily pads or other plants and grasses. Often we stumbled across snakes, sometimes water moccasins, that had entered our sample area for a feast. And then there were the alligators that had come for food also. These critter encounters were no problem when working from the safety of the boat, but while wading around up to your armpits in the river of grass they could be quite intimidating! I had several close calls with poisonous snakes and aggressive alligators that for some time caused reoccurring nightmares.

Shocking Stories

Our next best fish-sampling tool was the electro-shocking boat and we used this day and night and on an array of projects around the Everglades. My very first experience was undoubtedly my most exciting. Walt and I were conducting night sampling for largemouth bass along the L29 canal which paralleled the Tamiami Trail. I was in the bow controlling the foot pedal while Walt ran the boat. We had captured several nice bass for a tagging project and had placed them in our live box. It was pretty dark and our boat lights had limited range. As we proceeded along the edge of the canal about ten feet from shore a huge alligator slid off the bank and glided out just in front of the boat less than five feet in front of me. "Hit him," Walt called out. I hit the foot pedal and there was a tremendous explosion of water, weeds, and gator ending up nearly in my lap! I was soaked and scared out of my wits. I looked back and there was Walt having one of the best laughs of his life. Of all my Everglades adventures this was one of the most frightening!

An airboat heads down the Tamiami Trail Canal (L39), site of my first big gator encounter.

We had learned from this experience and others like it that the fish shocker did a pretty dang good job on alligators. Our coworkers in the Game Division got wind of this and talked me into helping them capture gators for a tagging study. For the next year or so I took the game biologists out into the Everglades at night in the shocker boat and helped them capture alligators up to about six feet long for tagging. Anything larger was left for den tagging, where the operation could be conducted more safely. Once an occupied den was located, usually one of the half crazed game wardens volunteered to "go in," while the more educated and seasoned game biologists would stay back to relative safety. The game warden guys were pretty fearless, much like Australia's Crocodile Hunter, the late Steve Irwin. After entering the den they tied a rope around the gators tail and attached the other end to the bumper of a "half track" or "swamp buggy." The gator was pulled out of the den and then jumped on first by the game wardens, second by the game biologists, and last by the most sane of the crew—a brave fisheries biologist! After hog-tying the gator we took measurements and applied a couple of different tags before it was released. Unfortunately, this all happened in the days before hazardous-duty pay became common!

Once while conducting a shocker survey along the North New River Canal, which paralleled State Road 84, we captured several snook along with the targeted bass. Instead of releasing them back into the canal, where they had access back to their normal saltwater environs, we decided to conduct an unauthorized experiment. We kept a dozen snook in our live box and transported them back to Tigertail Rockpit, a small enclosed freshwater pond located near town. We had stocked the pond with bass and bluegills and were fertilizing the pond as part of a growth rate study. Although we had no idea whether snook would survive in a totally freshwater environment, we knew that they had plenty to eat! One year later we decided to rotenone the pond to assess the production of bass and bluegills. To our surprise, all our snook had survived and had obtained exceptional growth! I don't know if this finding was ever applied to Florida's freshwater fish stocking program, but it certainly should have been.

Sandra with a nice snook taken while night fishing at Port Everglades.

The pay was pretty low in Florida but there were a few fringe benefits that helped even things out. The main one was the personal use of the state boat on my days off. I would take the family out for tours of the Intercoastal Waterway and friends out fishing in the Everglades during the day for bass and to Port Everglades for snook fishing at night. Since the best way to fish for snook at night was with live mullet, what better way to capture mullet than with the shocker boat? In the early evening we would cruise up and down the canals adjacent to Port Everglades capturing mullet with the shocker boat and then run out to the Port entrance and anchor up for snook fishing later that night. We caught snook up to 30-pounds and enjoyed eating every ounce. I still rate snook right up there with halibut as one of the best eating fish I have ever had.

Taking the family for a ride in "Daddy's Airboat" near Andytown, Florida. L. to R; Sandra, Laurie, Loren, and a neighbor friend holding Mitch.

Fishing and Tagging

During my first year on the job we got hooked up with the Schlitz Brewing Company in a largemouth bass tagging project. We captured bass for this project using the shocker boat and by sportfishing. I put in several hundred hours of paid sport fishing over a two-year period on this project. Although the shocker boat worked well in the canals that bordered and drained the Everglades, it was not an effective tool back in the heavily vegetated marsh areas. Nor would netting work well in these back country areas. So, we *reluctantly* (ha!) determined that sportfishing was our best tool for capturing bass for tagging. Our technique was to airboat back into a large, relatively open and thus fishable slough and exit the airboat on the upwind side. The airboat was then allowed to drift down to the far end of the slough as we began our *wade fishing* in the same direction. We would stringer any bass we caught to our waists and later empty them into a live box that sat in the airboat at the end of the slough. After a day of fishing we weighed, measured, tagged and then released the bass we had caught. On a good day of *work* we might tag and release 30-to-40 Florida largemouth bass.

Weedless lures were essential, as were stiff rods and a strong line. Our rods and lines changed, but our reels were Ambassador 5000s. Almost exclusively we used just two lures: Johnson spoons and Weedwings. These were almost always tipped with either a pork rind chunk or strip, usually Uncle Josh's. Walt and I caught several hundred largemouth bass while fishing on the job in our years together in the Everglades. The largest bass we caught in these shallow, weed- choked waters were in the ten- pound class. We caught dozens of bass in the 5- to- 9 pound class while wading around fighting off alligators and water moccasins. We caught and released several gators in the 2- to- 4 foot class on sport fishing gear but didn't mess with anything larger. I think with the snakes we were both just plain lucky to avoid getting struck.

Swim Fast, or Die

We did have one close call with a gator that haunted me afterward for a long time. Our airboat had broken down one afternoon two miles back into the marsh in Conservation Area lll about five miles south of the Miami Canal. It was in the late afternoon and during the cold of winter. Neither of us was dressed for a night out in the cold, which got down into the thirties in January, nor did we have any extra food or other survival gear. Our airboat had been dependable and although we usually carried a radio, it was on the blink. Our two choices were to (1) spend the night sitting and freezing in the airboat with no rescue likely until the next day or (2) walk out through two miles of waist-deep Everglades, swim a 100-foot-wide canal at dusk, and then walk the five miles back to the car in the dark. We chose the latter option since we were already cold and we both leaned toward an active versus a passive solution to our predicament.

It took more than two hours to wade to the edge of the 12- foot deep canal and we arrived about a half hour after sunset. The swim across the canal would have been a piece of cake, except for one rather large problem. One of the largest American alligators either of us had ever encountered was lying on the bank, head toward us, on the opposite side of the canal! Real fear struck deeply in my gut. Walt was speechless for a minute except for a softly muttered "Oh, s——!" Finding our way back to the airboat in the dark was not an option. Spending the night standing waist-deep in the marsh was not an option either as we were both aware of a condition called hypothermia! We had to swim the canal, gator or no gator. We discussed whether to swim slowly and quietly or to make an Olympic-style dash. We were only about 100 feet down the canal from the gator and could go no farther due to a heavy stand of sawgrass. Slinking quietly into the edge of the canal we started out with a quiet and slow dogpaddle across, all the time with our eyes fixed on our would be predator. We had made it perhaps 20- feet across the 100-foot-wide canal when the gator sensed our presence and slid off the bank into the water on the other side. There is no category in the Olympics for an 80-foot swim, but if there was, Walt and I would be co-record holders! We were across that canal and to the safety of the levee in nanoseconds. We half-walked, half-jogged the five miles back to the car. It was near midnight when we reached the tavern in Andytown. Instead of our usual end-of-the-day Falstaff or Schlitz, Walt and I downed a couple of hot buttered rums. We carried a functional radio and overnight survival gear on our airboat after that!

———

Andy, the Andytown Menace.

Old Andy, as he was known, was an impressive and relatively tame alligator in the 8- to- 9 foot class. He had taken up residence in a small pond immediately adjacent to one of the gas stations along the west side of Highway 27 in Andytown. Andy had grown somewhat accustomed to being fed whatever scraps people wanted to discard as they stopped to gas up and perhaps try to get a closeup picture of an alligator. Walt and I sometimes stopped by and while gassing up the airboat threw Andy a few fish from one of our rotenone samples. One day as I was at the station checking oil in the airboat, a beautiful new white Cadillac with New York license plates pulled up to the gas pumps. While Mr. Caddy watched over the station attendant, the Mrs., dressed to the nines, unloaded the family's prized white curly-haired poodle from the back seat of the Caddy. Judged by its rhinestone collar and demeanor, it must have been a show dog. I was somewhat mesmerized by the total scene, which was sort of like Bloomingdale's arriving in the middle of the podunk Everglades pit stop of Andytown—or I might have been able to prevent the tragedy that was about to take place.

The decked-out, high-heeled Mrs. Caddy proceeded to walk her well-manicured show dog to the edge of the small pond, evidently for a drink of water and perhaps a poo. Mr. Caddy was in the process of asking me if there were any alligators in this area when the Mrs. let out a bloodcurdling scream. It was at that moment that I realized that Andy had not yet been fed that day. It was over in seconds. Andy was swimming away with the poodle clenched tightly between his teeth; the Mrs. left standing with leash and rhinestone collar in hand. I was impressed that she hadn't let go as the big gator snatched away her prized poodle at the pond's edge.

Running like a dog through the Everglades, skippin' like a frog through the slimy bog........ But you better keep moving and don't stand still, if the skeeters don't get you then the gators will. (Harlan Howard)

———

The Great Flood

During the summer of 1966 I got to witness firsthand a great environmental tragedy created by a combination of man's ignorance and nature's extremes. For years the Army Corps of Engineers had been ditching and diking the Everglades Conservation Areas south of Lake Okeechobee for flood control and to create more dry land for farming and other development. The natural water flow of the Everglades was altered to the extent that the contained conservation areas could not be drained rapidly enough when heavy rains occurred. Heavy rains came during the summer of 1966 and what took place was a man made disaster created with an assist from Mother Nature. Pump stations north of Conservation Area lll worked overtime in an effort to drain farmlands as the heavy summer rains continued. There were not enough culverts and spillways to drain the area, and more than 900 square miles of Everglades were flooded. Deer, wild hogs, raccoons, and other mammals sought out the relative safety of high ground, which consisted of hundreds of small islands known as "Deer Islands," scattered throughout the area. Trouble was, most of these islands were only two or three feet higher than the surrounding sloughs and after a while as the flood worsened, they also became flooded. Deer and hogs herded up on these small islands and the food supply was soon depleted. Starvation was inevitable unless something was done.

Great Everglades Deer Rescue

That's where yours truly came into the picture along with every other Florida Fish and Game biologist and technician south of Orlando! A state of emergency was declared and all available resources were called upon to mount the "Great Everglades Rescue." Our assignment, should we choose to accept it (no choice really), was to capture all the deer and wild hogs in the area and move them to drier areas to the north. At first it was fun and exciting; in the end it was pretty sad.

The great deer rescue started on August 3, 1966. The idea was to run these imperiled deer down with airboats and then lasso them. Two guys would then jump out of the airboat into the marsh to hog-tie and blindfold the deer. After loading back onto the airboat the deer were run back to one of the levees where they were loaded onto a helicopter and flown north to dry ground up near Lake Okeechobee. In some cases tranquilizers were used since the deer were obviously under great stress. At first the operation appeared to be working quite well, but within a day or two we had some hot weather and things took a turn for the worse. We lost some deer during the capture phase and then more during handling and transport. At the time no one knew for sure but it appeared to be a combination of the stress and heat that was causing the problem. Most of the deer transported out of the area and released died within a few days.

This phase of the operation was a complete failure. Autopsies performed on the deceased deer indicated most had died from heart failure due to stress with the heat, and in some cases tranquilizers contributed to the problem. You would never have known this from the press coverage at the time. A rosy picture was being painted each night on the TV news. The chief coordinator of the project would appear being interviewed by reporters as he sat in an airboat out in the middle of the glades. All was going well, according to the coordinator, and the project was a huge success. For me it was a first-hand introduction to creative news reporting and the term CYA (cover your ass).

The Hog Patrol

After a few days on the deer rescue project it was discovered that I had the largest and most powerful airboat involved in the operation. This newly constructed airboat was designed to haul heavy loads for our fisheries research project and at 14 feet by 7 feet and powered by a 230 hp Continental aircraft engine—this baby was a workhorse. Thus I was assigned to assist the Hog Patrol, Phase ll of the rescue project.

Introduced "wild" hogs were occupying and rooting up what dry land remained on the deer islands. Unlike the deer, they could have been fed and probably survived the flood, but the habitat destruction they were causing was severe and the decision was made to capture and remove them from the islands of Conservation Area lll. That was my assignment on the Hog Patrol. Our crew consisted of myself as airboat operator, game biologist Carl Divinyi (in charge of operation), game technician David Albury, and Louis Barton, a Fort Lauderdale High School student volunteer.

The hog traps were large 10-by-10 foot heavy steel pens. We transported these by airboat to the islands occupied by hogs, set them up, and then baited them with a sack of corn. Quite often by the next day we had captured every hog on the island. We then jumped into the pen, wrestled and hog-tied the smaller ones, and loaded them into the boat. The larger hogs were another matter. These were lassoed first, wrestled down, blinded with a gunnysack, and then hog-tied. It took all four of our crew to manage the bigger hogs and we were covered from head to toe with mud, blood, and pig poop by the end of the day!

Charged!

On one memorable occasion we were all standing around outside of a pen getting ready to "go in" when someone yelled out "RUN!" Out of the brush about fifteen yards away came charging the biggest and meanest boar any of us had witnessed to date. With 7-inch tusks flashing in the sun this nearly 400-pound giant black boar chased the four of us to a large palmetto palm tree on the back side of the pen where we were able to fend it off. Carl didn't want anything else to do with this monster hog, so we left the island that day without further effort to capture it.

David Albury was cut out of the fearless game warden cloth and was determined to capture this hog. A few days later he talked one of the other airboat operators into bringing him back to Hog Head and David, with just a big stick in hand, chased the big hog off the island and into 4 feet of sawgrass swamp. Half swimming, half wading, he caught up with the slow moving hog. He then dove under water, grabbed it by its two rear ankles, and hung on for dear life. By holding it in this manner he was able to avoid the razor-sharp tusks. After wrestling it in the water for awhile, he, and the airboat operator, struggled to load it onboard. Unfortunately, after they hog-tied and secured it to the boat, the big hog died a short time later. This was probably due to combination of near drowning and heart failure induced by the stress of the struggle, according to David.

Everglades Mapping Project

By the spring of 1966 I had spent two and one half years running around Everglades Conservation Area lll in an airboat, power boat, and four-wheel-drive Jeep. I had been to all corners of the area and at the time probably knew my way around as well as anyone. Conservation Area lll was huge—about 40 miles long from north to south and averaging about 23 miles in width for a total area of approximately 915 square miles. Yet there was no map of this region showing the location of airboat trails and, of the approximately 40 cabins that were scattered throughout the area. So in June 1966 I set about to rectify this situation with my second "Great Map Project." (my first map was of the Elmwood River in Massachusetts).

Since at first this was not an official Florida Game and Fresh Water Fish Commission project, I had few resources with which to work. I started out with an outline of the area and filled in the airboat trails and cabin locations with which I was most familiar. While I was working in the Everglades on fisheries projects or just fishing or hunting on my own, I ran compass direction on the various trails and then used a speed and time relationship to estimate distance. I plotted island and cabin locations using the same technique. After a few months I came up with a draft map which I took around to major users of the area, including game wardens, cabin owners, fishers and hunters,

Miccosukee Indians, and finally alligator poachers and froggers. I received opinions on the accuracy of the trails and cabin locations and then adjusted my map according to the majority or to those I held in greatest respect. A highly scientific project to this point, yet a start!

As the map project progressed, I was able to pick up some support and encouragement from the FGFWFC, for whom I worked. Budgets were pathetically small back then, so the best I could do was finagle an aerial survey by helicopter over the area. We spent several hours checking my trail and cabin locations as well as relative distances, which I was then able to "ground-truth" with my draft map. The end result was a good one and I never received any complaints on the accuracy of the final Everglades map. Just kudos.

Walt and I had conducted some of the fisheries and environmental studies for a new highway that was to traverse the heart of Everglades Conservation Area III. My map was probably the first published to ever show the location of this new Florida highway—Alligator Alley. Years later in Alaska I met and worked with one of the more infamous Everglades alligator

Wade fishing for snook along the Intercoastal Waterway near Fort Lauderdale often produced nice fish like this one.

poachers from the '60s, one Til Thompson. Til flew me around Cook Inlet in his Super Cub on numerous salmon and herring surveys during the '70s. Til told me that after my map was published in 1967, no self-respecting Everglades alligator poacher ever left home without it! The map was probably my main contribution to users of the Everglades, including some of the more notorious characters, from my three and one half years of work there. (The map is on page 36).

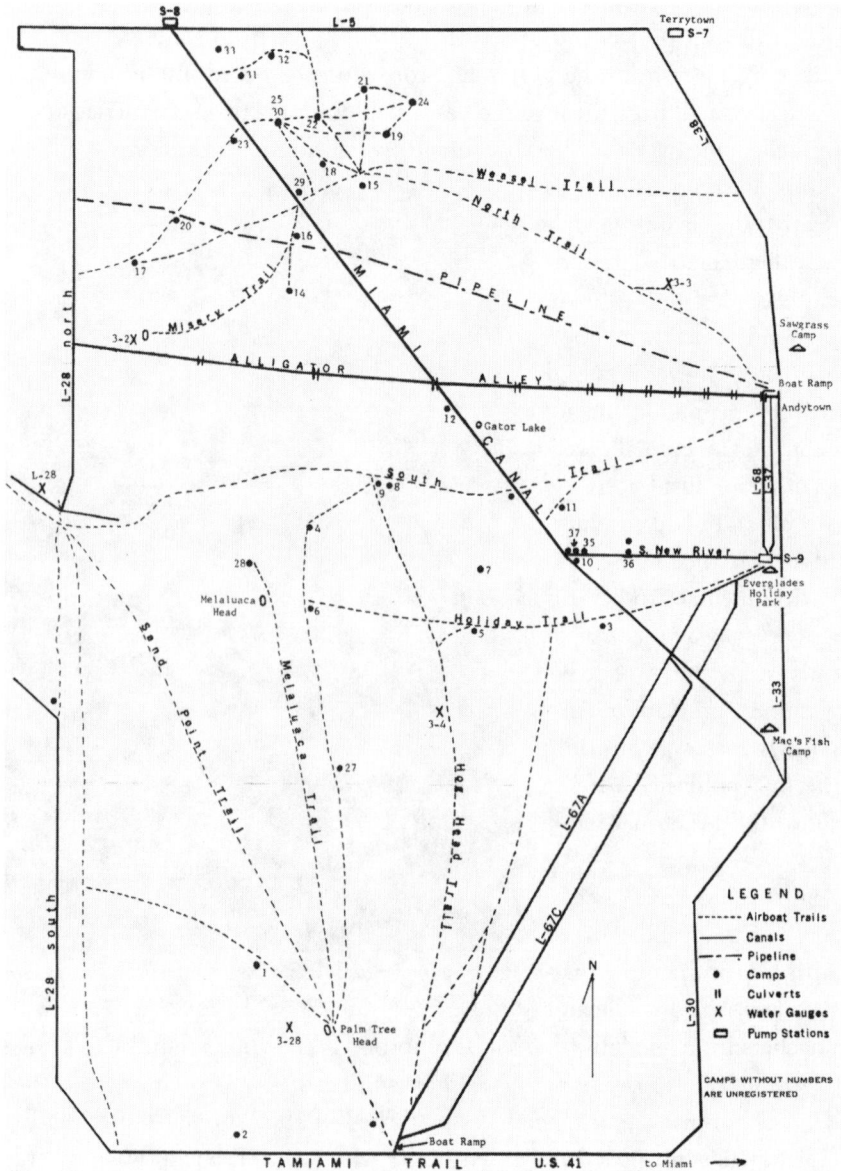

Everglades Conservation Area III. circa 1967

Chapter 6
Back to the Bay State

After three years of working in the excessive heat and humidity of South Florida and with water moccasins and gators as my constant companions, it was time for a change. Although I had enjoyed the work, Sandra and I had grown to dislike the climate, at least for about six months of the year. I applied for fisheries biologist positions in Alaska, Washington, and Massachusetts and then left Florida in June 1967 to return to the Bay State. While awaiting a job offer I worked as a grave digger in the Elmwood Cemetery and between the change in climate and working in cold, rainy weather I managed to come down with viral pneumonia! While recovering I received a job offer from the Massachusetts Division of Marine Fisheries at Sandwich on Cape Cod. I was hired as marine shellfish biologist with the Cape and North Shore as my main work areas.

I was hired by Frank Grice and assigned to work with Arnie Carr. Coastal towns in Massachusetts employ "shellfish wardens" to enforce shellfish regulations and to culture and enhance shellfish populations within their jurisdictions. The assignment for Arnie and me was to assist these wardens in assessing their respective shellfish populations and developing programs to expand and enhance these resources wherever possible. Our work included oyster culture through "rafting"; transplanting both seed and mature forms of bay scallops, soft shell and quahog clams; water quality sampling; and identification of potential culture sites. We also got involved in assessing impacts from an oil spill that occurred in a small saltwater lagoon in West Falmouth near Wood's Hole. This latter part of my job provided experience that would later prove valuable while I was employed as a biologist in Alaska.

Bluefish Bonanza

Arnie Carr proved not only to be a good boss, but also a great fishing partner. In the fall of 1967 Arnie and I entered the Martha's Vineyard Striped Bass and Bluefish Tournament. This is a pretty big event with a history dating back to 1913. Arnie supplied the boat, gear, and bait and I came along for the ride. Having never caught a big bluefish, Arnie thought I might provide a little beginner's luck. Little did he know! We were trolling along the edge of a rip in Nantucket Sound when the rod I was holding doubled over. We had been fishing less than an hour and I was hooked into what appeared to be a decent sized fish. After a battle of about 15-minutes, I landed a bluefish weighing 17 pounds, 4 ounces which Arnie thought could take first place in the tournament. We no sooner got our lines back in the water when Arnie hooked up and proceeded to land another huge bluefish, the same size as mine! We entered the bluefish and ended up taking first place in the tournament which was worth a $500 savings bond and some pretty high end fishing tackle.

Lobsters Galore

I didn't get a chance to work with lobsters in my shellfish biologist position. That duty was assigned to another biologist on a totally different project. So, although we had ample access to clams, scallops, and oysters for the dinner table, lobsters were not so easy to come by. And then we discovered a little-known provision in the Massachusetts Shellfish Regulations which permitted a licensed resident sport fisherman to fish up to five lobster pots for his own and his immediate family's use. We had been in the Bay State only a few months and had not yet acquired a boat, and at first this looked like it would present a formidable problem. Then one day Sandra and I were walking along the edge of the Cape Cod Canal when we observed a guy wading out into the canal at low tide and pulling on a rope. At the end of this rope was a wooden lobster trap (or pot) and lo and behold, it contained a half dozen legal-sized lobsters! This was a new fishery experience and it didn't take us long to round up the necessary gear and become Cape Cod Canal lobster fishermen.

At the time we lived in Monument Beach, just a couple of miles from the Railroad Bridge on the canal. After work we would wait for low tide in the canal and then go about setting out the traps. Besides the traps, line, and bait the only other gear needed was a pair of chest waders and a 10-foot pole. The technique involved wading out as far as possible at low tide with a baited trap, pushing it out over the drop-off with the pole, and then tying off the rope to one of the large rocks along the edge of the canal. The next evening we would go back at low tide and retrieve the traps. Voila—lobsters for the dinner table!

That fall of 1967 was a great time for culinary delights—all the seafood we could eat for free, and enough lobsters to provide friends and family. The season of bounty culminated with Sandra and I holding a huge New England style clambake in our backyard on Eel Pond in Monument Beach. To top off this wonderful day we all watched the "Impossible Dream" Red Sox of 1967 wrap up the American League Pennant.

Another Robert Frost Moment

Everything was going pretty well with me working for the Division of Marine Fisheries and our family living on a saltwater pond on Cape Cod. And then a telegram arrived unexpectedly from Alaska: "Would you be interested in a Fisheries Biologist ll position with the Alaska Department of Fish and Game? Starting salary of $903/month." At the time I was making about $500 per month and even the director of our division made much less than Alaska was offering. But money was not the driving force behind our decision to make the change—it was a call that said, "*Go north young man.*" I had been waiting eight years for this opportunity. My interest in Alaska had started when I was a sophomore in high school and an Elmwood lad, 19-or-20 years old, returned from his first year in Alaska, where he had been stationed with the U.S. Coast Guard. He had known of my interest in all things related to the outdoors including hunting, fishing, and trapping,

Author at Eel Pond in Monument Beach, Massachusetts, with 17 pound bluefish he caught fishing in Nantucket Sound.

and had brought back a few copies of Alaska Magazine for me to peruse. The seed was planted! From that time on I planned my life around an eventual move to Alaska.

During my senior year in high school I had written to Jim Brooks, then director of the Alaska Division of Game, and inquired about a possible position with ADF&G following my graduation. The letter I received back from Brooks basically said "Young man, you need to go to college, major in biology or wildlife management, and after graduation contact me again." I followed this advice and majored in wildlife biology at the UMASS. Four years later in the spring of my senior year at UMASS I wrote back to Mr. Brooks, informing him of my impending graduation, and asking for a position with ADF&G. The response I received this time basically said "Young man, what you need to do now is gain some experience working in the wildlife or fisheries field and then contact me again." And that I had done earlier in the spring when I reapplied to Alaska after gaining three and one half years of experience with Florida Fish and Game. This was now the second Robert Frost moment in my life where "two roads diverged in a wood and I—I took the one less traveled by, and that has made all the difference." There really wasn't any hesitation. Although everything was working out well in Massachusetts, I was destined to travel north with my family and make a life in Alaska.

Chapter 7
North to Alaska

I responded immediately to the telegram from Alaska and accepted a Fisheries Biologist ll position in Homer. Because I needed to report to duty by March 1, 1968, my dad and I took off in my fully loaded Dodge Sports van on February 11, and headed north. Sandra, Laurie, and Mitch were to follow after I got settled into housing in Homer. Dad had the typical unenlightened picture of Alaska in his mind—visions of igloos and frozen wasteland. He was confident enough to bet me a bottle of blackberry brandy (his favorite) that the temperature in Homer, upon our arrival, would be lower than that of our departure point in Elmwood, Massachusetts. Since I had read up on Alaska I was aware that Homer was in a kind of "banana belt" and was sometimes referred to as the "Summer Land of Alaska." And since the morning we hit the road to go north the temperature in Elmwood was hovering around zero, I knew I had a lock on this bet!

We traveled across the Trans Canada Highway and then up the Alaska Highway, or Alcan as it was called then. Roads were icy in February and we managed to slide off twice, once rolling over and ending up cab side down in a ditch! We reached the border on February 22, and stopped at the "Welcome to Alaska" sign. After reading through all the superlatives about Alaska on the sign I came to the final one at the bottom: "And there are no snakes in Alaska." Someone had hand engraved off to the side "Except Hickel." This was my introduction to Governor Walter Hickel and Alaska politics!

Dad and I arrived in Anchorage just in time for the first day of the Fur Rendezvous, an annual event held each February to celebrate the importance of fur trapping to the great state of Alaska. Attending the World Championship Sled Dog Race, we were surprised to learn that one of the top competitors in this event, Dr. Roland Lombard, was from our home state of Massachusetts!

Alaska would be full of surprises. As we cheered Dr. Lombard along Fourth Avenue to the finish of the race, Dad noticed for the first time that it was actually quite mild outside. "Damn it," he said, "You might win that bottle of blackberry brandy after all!" Sure enough, when we arrived in Homer the next day it was a balmy 40 degrees and on top of that there was very little snow to be seen. Dad's awakening to the realities of Alaska was now complete.

Meet the Boss

My Alaska experience got off to a good start since shortly after arriving in Homer I learned that I had one of the most knowledgeable Alaskan outdoorsmen and biologists as my immediate supervisor. Jim Rearden had been the first wildlife management professor at the University of Alaska in Fairbanks and had been hired as Area Management Biologist for Cook Inlet commercial fisheries shortly after Alaska became a state. Jim turned out to be the best teacher and boss I had during my 25-year professional career. Jim, and his wife Audrey, insisted that Dad and I spend a few nights with them until I was able to find housing suitable for my family. There wasn't much at all on the rental market at the time but within a couple of days I had found a large three-bedroom home for the reasonable rate of $150 per month. It turned out that this home was poorly insulated and could not be adequately heated in cold weather. But hey, it was already springtime in Alaska, or so it seemed at this time in early March.

Family Reunited

Dad returned home in early March and proudly showed movie films to our family of our trip up the Alaska Highway, of the Anchorage Fur Rendezvous, and of beautiful green downtown Homer, Alaska. The grass was green and there was no snow in sight around our yard out East End Road in Homer at the time Dad had left in mid-March. Sandra and the kids left from Boston and flew to Anchorage on March 23, where I was to pick them up and drive them down to Homer. They were fully expecting to arrive to spring-like conditions and thus were surprised when they learned I couldn't pick them up in Anchorage because the road had been closed due to a snowstorm. Yes, Alaska was full of surprises and this one was rude—nearly two feet of snow falling in late March! After a few phone calls Sandra and the kids were able to get a flight on Western Airlines from Anchorage to Homer. As I greeted the family to wintry conditions at the Homer airport with "Welcome to springtime in Alaska," my wife gave me a somewhat puzzled look.

We toughed out the rest of the spring in our rather cool house, but by fall had located more suitable housing for the coming winter.

Chapter 8
Cook Inlet Management

My new position was titled Assistant Area Biologist and the area I was assigned to was Cook Inlet. This was a huge area, about the size of New York state, yet there were only three biologists responsible for commercial fisheries management in the area. Jim was the Area Biologist, Don Stewart was the assistant responsible for Upper Cook Inlet (UCI), and I was the assistant assigned to Lower Cook Inlet (LCI). The LCI area included all waters south of Anchor Point, west to Kamishak Bay, south to the Barren Islands, and then east to a point beyond Seward and Resurrection Bay.

Cook Inlet had commercial fisheries for five species of salmon, five species of shrimp, three species of crab, and for herring, halibut, scallops, and razor clams. Over time I would become involved in the man-

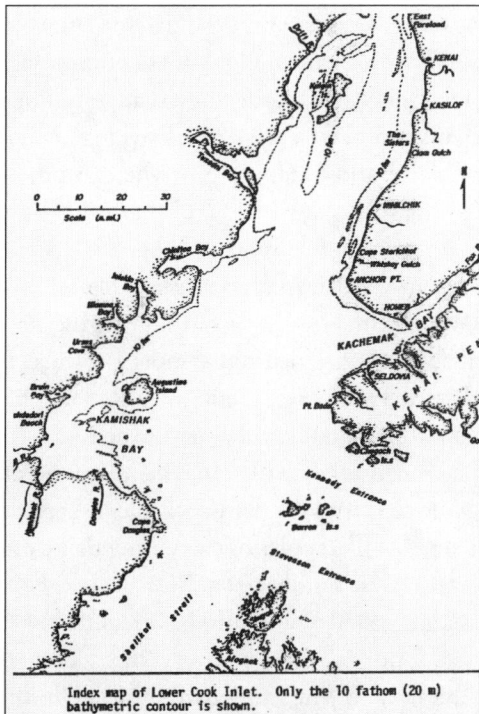

Index map of Lower Cook Inlet. Only the 10 fathom (20 m) bathymetric contour is shown.

Map of Cook Inlet showing locations of Homer, Kachemak Bay, and Kenai. (Map is from ADF&G report cited in Sources)

agement of all of these species except halibut, which were managed by the International Pacific Halibut Commission. In addition to the management team in 1968, we also had one research biologist, Al Davis, for the entire Cook Inlet area. Al's work was primarily involved with salmon, and the only shellfish research being conducted at the time was done by the National Marine Fisheries Service out of the Kasitsna Bay Lab located across Kachemak Bay.

King of the Crab

The only commercial fishery going on in Kachemak Bay at the time I started work out of Homer in late February 1968, was the king crab fishery. In the late '60s and early '70s Kachemak Bay was producing about 1.5 million pounds of king crab annually. I had been "on board" with ADF&G about a week when my boss, Jim Rearden, told me, "We need to know what's going on out there on the fishing grounds. I hear they may be catching and dumping a lot of soft-shell crab. I want you to go out on some of the crab boats and see what those guys are up to. We may need to close them down." This was my first assignment—to go out on the king crab boats, observe their operations, and collect the data necessary to determine whether they should be closed down or allowed to continue fishing. The only problem was that this fishery was worth more than a million dollars to the local economy and that I had never even seen a live king crab! I had been in Alaska only a couple of weeks and I was the guy who was potentially going to be responsible for closing this industry down.

And that's exactly what happened and how I got off to a rather infamous start in my career as an Alaska fisheries biologist. On my first trip on a crab boat out of Homer I went out on the *Royal Lady* with "Red" Calhoun, an affable and grizzled old skipper who had several years of experience fishing the waters of Lower Cook Inlet. Red taught me everything there was to know about king crab and I soon learned how to identify the soft-shell crab. Red, like Jim, was concerned that handling too many of these soft-shelled king crab while targeting the hard-shelled crab for market, was harmful to the resource. I kept detailed notes of everything that came up in the crab pots—number of legal males, number of sub-legal males, number of females, number of egg-bearing females, and number of soft-shell crab. After a second trip out to the crab grounds, this time with Max Devany on the *Betty Lou,* I turned all my data over to Jim and based on these findings he issued an emergency order closing the king crab fishery down.

Since this was the only bay fishery going on at the time, the closure had a big impact on both Homer and Seldovia, a small fishing community located across

Kachemak Bay. Although most of the Homer-based fishermen supported the closure for conservation purposes, some of the skippers in Seldovia were up in arms over this action. As the new kid on the block, I took a good share of the blame. After that the Seldovia skippers always delighted in trying to get me as seasick as possible whenever I went out as an observer on their crab boats.

To top it off, about two weeks later I was responsible for doing the same thing to another king crab fishery, this one located in Kamishak Bay on the west side of Cook Inlet. After making three trips to Kamishak, two aboard the *Aleutian Queen* and one on the *Bessie M*, this fishery was closed by emergency order. While serving as an observer on these trips I would on occasion endure comments as to whether or not I would make good crab bait! Such was my introduction to Cook Inlet commercial fisheries management.

Humpy Heaven

Of the five species of salmon in the Cook Inlet area, pink salmon, also called humpies, are the most numerous and most important commercially around Kachemak Bay and the Outer District. They spawn in most of the

Commercial Fisheries biologists Ken Roberson and Al Davis, sampling for pre-emergent pink salmon fry in Humpy Creek.

salmon streams that extend from Kachemak to Resurrection Bay. The major pink salmon streams in Kachemak Bay area are Humpy Creek, Tutka, Seldovia, and Port Graham. The escapement in these four streams in the late '60s and early '70s was averaging about 100,000 pinks.

My second assignment for ADF&G was to assist Al Davis, the salmon research biologist, in a sampling program designed to estimate the egg- to-fry, survival in these four streams. During the month of April we traveled to the streams by either boat or floatplane, landed at the mouth, and then hiked up the streams to a point where the farthest salmon had spawned. Our gear consisted of snowshoes, buckets, nets, and a backpack-mounted pump with hoses. We also carried some minimal survival gear. We worked our way downstream digging up the gravel at our designated sample sites, collecting and then counting the number of pink salmon fry that washed out. At times we encountered large areas of dead salmon eggs. These were usually in shallow areas along the stream margins and had simply frozen out. Following severe winters, such as the winter of 1970-1971, we sometimes encountered more dead than live eggs in these streams.

From the above technique, we were able to estimate the number of salmon fry per square meter that had survived the winter and this information was then used to forecast the adult return for the following year. (All pink salmon return as adults the year following their emergence as fry from the spawning stream).

Salmon Management 101

I spent six seasons in salmon management in the Cook Inlet area. Although most of my time during the first five years was allocated to the Lower Cook Inlet (LCI) seine fishery, as time went on I got more and more involved with the Upper Cook Inlet (UCI) gill net fishery. In LCI, salmon management was quite simple compared to UCI. Most of the salmon streams in LCI are clear-water streams and salmon can be easily seen and thus counted by using either a ground or aerial survey. In some cases, like Port Dick in the Outer District, a salmon-counting weir was used. Each of the major salmon streams had an escapement goal based on the amount of spawning area available. Using the past history of run timing, we simply balanced the number of salmon observed in the stream on any given date with a total return projection based on this run timing. For example, if a stream had an escapement goal of 30,000 and we had 10,000 already in the stream by late July, we could be pretty much assured that by the end of August we would meet our total escapement goal of 30,000. The stream observations were just one part of the decision making process. We also looked at effort, catch, and numbers of salmon observed out in the clear-water bays. During the fishing season we opened and closed different bays frequently by emergency order (E.O.) and moved "closed waters" markers in or out away from the stream mouths as the strength of the return dictated. This was always a fine balancing act, but it's a successful system used throughout the state.

Walking salmon streams to obtain spawner counts also required the senior biologist with the survey crew to be a "bear guard."

Paved with Shrimp

In the spring of 1969, the Westinghouse Corporation sent a team to Homer to test out a new underwater TV system in the clear and productive waters of Kachemak Bay. Little did we know at the time just how productive this bay was and this little two-day venture really opened our eyes. This was the first of several underwater TV surveys of the bay which were to follow. We suspended the camera and lighting about seven feet off the bottom and proceeded to drift along in the test boat at various locations and depths in Kachemak Bay. At times we drifted along for minutes on end without ever seeing the bottom even though the lighting was good. Sometimes it was clouds of plankton that obscured visibility, but mostly I remember the unbelievable clouds of shrimp. Kachemak Bay supports five species of shrimp, but two were predominant— pink and humpy shrimp. As we drifted along, the schools of shrimp, hanging just off the bottom, were so thick that you virtually could not see the bottom of the bay for minutes on end. This biological phenomenon was not just in a few isolated areas of the bay but rather over extensive areas and at various bottom depths.

There hadn't been a major fishery for shrimp in Kachemak Bay prior to this time; in fact, the average catch for the previous ten years had been less than a half million pounds. Market conditions had improved by 1969 and a new shrimp-processing facility had opened on the Homer Spit. This was the year the shrimp fishery was going to take off, but I don't think anyone realized the true potential of the bay until this underwater survey was conducted. Over the next several years the trawl shrimp catch in Kachemak Bay averaged about five million pounds annually—in fact, that's the level at which the shrimp quota was eventually set. The processor, Alaskan Seafoods, set daily quotas for the shrimp boats in order to maintain product quality and keep up with processing capacity. It varied somewhat but was usually set at a daily catch of about 10,000 pounds per boat, and there were normally three or four boats delivering to the processor. As the shellfish management biologist, I sometimes accompanied the boats as an observer and took samples of the catch. Seldom did it take one of the trawlers more than an hour or two of fishing to obtain their daily quota and on one of these trips 12,500 pounds of pure *Pandalids*, 95 percent pink and humpy shrimp, was taken in a 20-minute trawl!

Sockeye Symphony

Although I had been assigned mainly to Lower Cook Inlet, over time I became more and more involved in Upper Cook Inlet salmon management. Whereas LCI was all about pink salmon, in UCI the sockeye, or red salmon, was the "money fish." The main producers of sockeye in UCI were the Kenai, Kasilof, and Susitna River systems. Since these UCI rivers were glacial, the aerial and ground counting techniques used in LCI could not be utilized for management purposes. Prior to 1966, the only in-season estimator of sockeye run strength was the commercial catch. There was no critical escapement information since the fish could not be seen in the glacial water. That is, until 1966.

Sonar Development

Jim Rearden had been a sonar operator in WWII and was convinced that migrating salmon could be counted using this technology. In 1964 Commissioner Walt Kirkness gave Jim the go-ahead to contract for a test project. The Bendix Corporation received the contract and assigned Al Menin to the project. By 1966 Menin, working with ADF&G personnel, had developed a prototype salmon sonar counter. In the summer of 1966, sonar counters were first tried in the Kenai River and by 1968 they were being used for management in both the Kenai and Kasilof River systems. Sonar for the Susitna River came a few years later. The sonar counters gave biologists a much needed in-season tool to estimate salmon escapement into the major river systems. Better decisions could now be made regarding allotted fishing time in Cook Inlet.

The 50 Foot Rule

In the major clear-water rivers of Bristol Bay, migrating sockeye had for years been observed from aerial surveys and counting towers. Without exception, these fish had moved up the rivers along, and within 50-feet of the riverbanks. Early on, it was not known if this behavior would be the same in the glacial waters of the Kenai and Kasilof rivers, so one of my jobs in the late '60s was to help determine this. Al Davis and his crew had installed the sonar array 50-feet out into the Kenai River from the banks on both the north and south side of the river at River Mile 19. One of my helpers and I floated down the middle of the river between the two sonar arrays with a 100 foot gill net at periodic intervals throughout the sockeye migration in an attempt to assess whether any sockeye were traveling outside the counters. In two years of doing this we caught only one sockeye outside the sonar target area, so we knew that our counting system was sound.

Test Fishing

The other program I was responsible for was Kenai and Kasilof River test fishing. We needed to have some method of "ground-truthing" the sonar counters during the first two or three years of operation until we had fine-tuned the use of these counters and could feel more confident in relying upon them for management decisions. I oversaw the test fish program which was conducted in the lower portions of the Kenai and Kasilof rivers during the late '60s and early '70s. We fished a 100-foot gill net in a consistent manner for two hours on each incoming tide at our test fish site. The catch of sockeye was used as an indicator of the relative migration of fish into the river that day. We were able to match up our best days of catch with the highest days of counting at the sonar which was located a few miles further upriver.

UCI Aerial Surveys.

Another component of our UCI in-season management involved aerial surveys of the commercial fishery during the open fishing periods. We flew a float plane out of Homer to count and observe the catch in the set nets fishing along the east side of the inlet and around Kalgin Island. Boat counts, area of fishing effort, and catch observations were also made for the 500 plus boat Cook Inlet drift gill-net fleet. Information from these surveys, a 4-wheel-drive beach survey, test fishing, sonar counts, and the cannery and tender reports—were all compiled by the end of the day. Based on all this current information, historical fishing patterns, and the feeling in your gut—a decision was made on the amount of fishing time and the area to be fished for the next fishing period. Jim Rearden always described this decision-making process in Cook Inlet as "management by the seat of your pants!"

Transition

Jim Rearden retired in 1970 and after two years of sitting in the Cook Inlet Area Biologist hot seat, Don Stewart, who had taken his place, was totally burned out and had transferred to a regional assistant position in Anchorage. Cook Inlet had always been totally understaffed in both the management and research divisions and had become known as being "impossible to manage." Following the 1971 salmon season in UCI, a million-dollar lawsuit had been filed against ADF&G for "mismanagement" of the sockeye return. Only one district-wide fishing period had been allowed at the peak of the run in 1971, and the total sockeye catch for the season was a record low of only 650,000.

The 1972 season wasn't much better, and on top of the poor sockeye returns there were now king salmon problems. Set net fishermen along the beaches were accused of intercepting too many king salmon and the streams in the Northern District, which included the Susitna River drainage, were not getting adequate escapement. More than half the population of Alaska lived in the Southcentral region and utilized Cook Inlet rivers and streams for sport, personal use, and subsistence fishing. More demands were being made on the resource and on the department, especially the Commercial Fisheries Division. Cook Inlet commercial fisheries management had become a nightmare.

Area Biologist for just two years, Don Stewart had left for a different position in Anchorage. I had immediately made it known that I had no interest in the position; in fact, I no longer wanted to remain in management and had already lined up another position with the newly created FRED Division. (Fisheries Rehabilitation Enhancement & Development). The department advertised the opening for the Cook Inlet Commercial Fisheries Area Biologist position statewide—and not one person applied! This had never happened before, since most Fisheries Biologist lll positions in the state were much coveted as a logical advancement for the many FB ll's employed by ADF&G at the time. Such was the reputation that went with this job!

Out of a Bind; Into the Fire!

Early in August 1972 I received a call on my birthday from ADF&G Commissioner Jim Brooks, and it wasn't to wish me a happy birthday! Brooks said "I want you to help me out of a bind and take the Cook Inlet Area Biologist position." I told him, as I had told my regional supervisor, Ken Middleton, that I had no interest in taking this position and had, in fact, already accepted a new job with Bob Roys, Director of the FRED Division. Brooks made it clear that he would block my advancement to this new position and reiterated that he needed me to take the commercial fisheries area biologist position. I asked him what would happen if I refused and he said, "It won't be good for your career!"

And so I became area biologist for Cook Inlet, against my wishes but probably best for my career. Jim Brooks owed me big time—and I never let him forget it! I did the best I could but never really liked the job and planned my getaway from day one. The pressure cooker that was Cook Inlet did not fit my personality well. While in the position I lobbied hard for additional money and staff so that the inlet could be managed more professionally. I also recommended to my supervisors that Cook Inlet be divided into two management areas—Upper Cook Inlet and Lower Cook Inlet—and that separate management and research staffs be assigned to each area. I even indicated that I would stay on and take one of the new positions if this change was made. When this recommendation was initially turned down, I began looking for an alternative.

I was much more interested in and better suited for research and that's where I headed at the first opportunity. The big break that would get me out of commercial fisheries management came just 15 months later, when "Big Oil" came to Kachemak Bay.

Chapter 9
Kachemak Bay Marine Research

I had been involved in a study to assess the impacts from an oil spill to a salt marsh in Falmouth, Massachusetts in 1967, so when I started work for ADF&G out of Homer in 1968 I soon became the go-to-guy for oil spills in Cook Inlet. Between 1968 and 1973, I had responded to several oil spills around Cook Inlet including two from large oil tankers. I had also been responsible for preparing ADF&G comments on pending oil lease sales and other oil and gas activities around the inlet. Normally the department was given a minimum of 30 days to comment on these activities.

The "boys"[1] over at the Department of Natural Resources (DNR), Oil and Gas Division, knew that any attempt to sell oil and gas leases in Lower Cook Inlet, and especially Kachemak Bay, would be highly controversial and as a result tried to rush through a sale for the area and by so doing subvert the public process. In late October, 1973, I was given just two days to comment on the proposed sale, instead of the usual 30 days. My comments documented the resources of the bay and their value to fishermen and the economy of the area. I recommended that Kachemak Bay be excluded from the sale. ADF&G backed this position but DNR ignored the recommendation and went ahead and held the sale anyway. A group of commercial fishermen and other citizens in Homer petitioned (300 signatures) DNR for a public hearing prior to the scheduled sale but were denied. The sale was held on December 13, 1973 and turned out to be the largest oil and gas lease sale in terms of revenue to the state since the Prudhoe Bay sale in 1969.

(1) Commissioner of Natural Resources, Charles Herbert; Director Oil and Gas Division, Homer Burrell; and Director Division of Lands, Pedro Denton.

More about the sale and subsequent buyback of the leases appears in the next chapter; however, this chapter will cover the marine research program that was initiated in Kachemak Bay as a direct result of the lease sale and surrounding controversy. The state legislature appropriated $300,000 for a study of the marine environment of Kachemak Bay and Lower Cook Inlet and the potential impact to the environment from oil and gas activities. In the spring of 1974, I was appointed to be field project leader for these studies. Dr. Pat Wennikens was appointed to administer this program and later Lance Trasky was added to our team as a habitat biologist. We were all under the Habitat Division with Pat and Lance working out of the Anchorage office and me out of Homer.

Kachemak Bay Marine Study Plan

By April 1974, we had developed a study plan, and the Legislature had appropriated funds to start the project. The program was specifically designed to assemble existing information concerning the effects of oil on biological resources, and to obtain information on biological resources of Kachemak Bay and their sensitivity to the impacts of oil development. The information gained would be used to provide a rational basis for regulation and enforcement activities during oil and gas exploration, development, and production.

Field work was initiated in August 1974 and continued through October 1976. The field studies were designed to identify the physical processes that control the movement of pollutants and larval marine life, and to provide baseline data on the biological resources of Kachemak Bay and Lower Cook Inlet. To reach these goals, the Marine and Coastal Habitat Division of ADF&G utilized both department biologists and contractors from three universities and two private consulting firms. New equipment and techniques were developed to determine current patterns and distribution of early life stages of king crab.

At the conclusion of the project we published a report, *Environmental Studies of Kachemak Bay and Lower Cook Inlet*, consisting of twelve volumes covering the entire scope of our project. Included were studies of circulation patterns, coastal morphology, distribution of larval crab and shrimp, benthic reconnaissance, marine plant and salt marsh communities, beach drift composition, hydrocarbons in intertidal environments, distribution and abundance of marine birds, and the potential impact of oil in the Kachemak Bay environment.

My job, in addition to helping design and implement these studies, was to oversee, and in many cases help conduct, the field portion of these studies. This work went on for three field seasons and was largely supported by two state vessels, the *MV Pandalus* and *MV Puffin*. The scope of the program was large and we learned a great deal of oceanographic and biological information about Kachemak Bay, helping us to understand how the bay functioned.

Keys to Productivity

We discovered that one of the keys to the high productivity of the bay was the presence of two large current gyres in the outer bay off Bluff Point. These gyres acted as a kind of trap for larval forms of crab and shrimp, enabling these early life forms to develop and then settle to the bottom of the bay, instead of being washed out and away into the lower inlet and eventually, to the Gulf of Alaska. Another key to the high productivity of the bay was an extremely high plankton production due to just the right mix of clear saline water with minerals, such as silica, provided by glacial runoff in the upper bay.

Another indication of Kachemak Bay's richness was discovered in the marine plant communities located mainly along the south side of the bay. Marine plant communities in general are highly diverse and among the most productive biological systems on earth. Marine biologists Rick Rosenthal and Dennis Lees from Dames and Moore environmental consulting firm concluded in their report that the kelp community along the south side of Kachemak Bay epitomized this concept. They reported that "countless numbers of organisms on both a transitory and year-round basis take advantage of the habitat provided by these plant communities. More than 100 plant species and 250 animal species were identified during this study."

Benthic Study

The study of marine life on the bottom of the bay provided another piece to the Kachemak Bay productivity pie. The benthic study utilized both substrate samples and underwater TV observations. Outer Kachemak Bay was found to be an area of considerable diversity and abundance of marine life. In addition to the commercially important species of crab and shrimp, more than 200 animal taxa were identified from samples collected in the outer bay. A shell debris assemblage on the shelf off Bluff Point on the northern side of the bay was the richest area sampled with more than 80 percent of the total number of species found there.

Hydrocarbons

Our review of hydrocarbon studies, including the extensive studies conducted by the NMFS Auke Bay Lab, showed that many of the marine life forms found in Kachemak Bay, and especially the early life forms, were extremely sensitive to even very low levels of oil pollution. Several studies indicated that levels as low as 1-to-4 parts per million of Cook Inlet and Prudhoe Bay crude oil would cause mortality in many of the early life forms of commercially important salmon and shellfish species that inhabit Kachemak Bay.

Recommendations

After three years of study we prepared our final report. In the final section, Summary and Recommendations, we concluded: "The evidence gathered in this study indicates that Kachemak Bay is a highly critical element in the Lower Cook Inlet ecosystem. The substantial environmental damage which could result from significant oil spillage, chronic oil pollution, and other activities associated with petroleum exploration and development is not considered to be an acceptable risk in Kachemak Bay, and *it is recommended that no petroleum exploration or development be allowed in Kachemak Bay.*"

Chapter 10
Kachemak Bay Oil Lease Fiasco

The Department of Natural Resources (DNR) had rushed through the normal oil lease sale process, even denying Homer citizens a public hearing on the proposed Kachemak Bay sale. Held on December 13, 1973, the Kachemak Bay lease sale brought in nearly $25 million and was the second most profitable in state history following the Prudhoe Bay sale. Standard Oil of California had dominated this, the 28th oil and gas lease sale in state history, taking 17 tracts and paying $16.6 million. Other major bidders were Shell at $5.4 million and Texaco at $2.6 million. The tracts drawing the greatest interest happened to be smack in the middle of the most important crab breeding and rearing area in Cook Inlet!

Senate Hearing

Following the denial of a public hearing prior to the lease sale by DNR Commissioner Charles Herbert, the Senate Resources Committee, headed by Bob Palmer, held a hearing in Homer on February 23, 1974. About 170 Homer citizens attended the hearing. Prior to the start of the hearing, a group of commercial fishermen and I were discussing how to reverse this sale when our local state representative Clem Tillion joined us. I will never forget his words and advice to us at this time: "You cannot beat the Big O. They are just too big and powerful. All you can do is take some mayonnaise jars with you in your boats after they start drilling, and scoop up any signs for evidence. But be sure the jars are sterilized." Although Clem did not testify at this, the first of several hearings to come, he soon became actively involved in the subsequent fight and eventually supported the side of the fishermen. But his comments did reflect a common perception in Alaska at that time—*whatever Big Oil wants, Big Oil gets.*

Prior to the Senate Resources hearing, ADF&G Commissioner Jim Brooks and Habitat Chief Mike Smith had met with DNR Commissioner Herbert. I was told by Smith that the comments from my memo submitted just prior to the sale had been used at this meeting between the two commissioners, and that Brooks had told Herbert that his department *strongly recommends that Kachemak Bay be withdrawn from the lease sale.* I believe that Jim Brooks took a somewhat courageous stand at that time as he was not only going up against the desired direction of DNR, but also policy set by Governor Egan. I believe that Brooks had strong feelings about oil development in critical areas and was willing to take at least an initial stand against leasing in the bay. Perhaps the fact that Egan was in the last year of his term in office also came into play.

About this same time a group called "Citizens for a Better Community" was formed by Homer resident Richard Robinson. This group was formed undoubtedly for the purpose of fighting against the Kachemak Bay oil lease and had written to Commissioner Brooks in early January requesting information on Kachemak Bay and the effects of oil in the marine environment. Habitat Chief Mike Smith answered this letter for Brooks in early February and told Robinson that he was assigning me (Mr. Flagg) the task of "assembling the information you seek." He went on to say "Loren has an excellent background with the marine environment and I am confident he will be able to assist you to the fullest."

ADF&G'S Testimony

Little did I know at the time what this would involve, but I found out a short time later, when Mike called me and asked that I prepare ADF&G's testimony for the upcoming Senate Resources Committee hearing. I asked Mike how far I could go and how strong I could make the comments that he would deliver at the hearing. He said that as far as Commissioner Brooks and he were concerned I was running the show. "Right now you are the one setting policy on Kachemak Bay, so go ahead and write whatever you want." It seemed a little strange and somewhat uncomfortable at the time to be a state employee, and yet act in a capacity to potentially undermine a program that obviously had the support of the governor. Two driving forces behind my actions at that time were my strong personal feelings for the bay and the fact that I had the support of Commissioner Brooks and Habitat Director Mike Smith.

I prepared the ADF&G testimony for the hearing and pretty much followed the comments that I had originally submitted on the proposed lease sale. These comments had been critical of DNR, had highlighted the biological value of the bay, and in conclusion had recommended that no oil development take place. Mike Smith came to the hearing and although he did not use all my comments (some diplomacy was in order) he did support a two-year moratorium on drilling and proposed that Kachemak Bay be designated by the Legislature as a *Critical Habitat Area*. This idea caught fire and the committee soon adopted it as a legislative priority.

Fishermen and Residents Speak

Following Smith's presentation to the Senate Resources Committee, two powerful testimonies were given by local citizens that were to set the tone and stage for other hearings to follow. Jim Rearden, former area biologist for the Commercial Fisheries Division, Board of Fish and Game member, and outdoors editor for *Alaska Magazine*, led off the hearing. Jim documented his own experiences as he dealt with oil industry problems in Cook Inlet over a 10-year period. He related how he had been frequently called out to respond to oil spills in the inlet from platforms, tankers, pipelines, and other sources. He had worked closely with federal and state agencies charged with monitoring oil pollution during this time and noted that from 1962 to 1973 a total of 260 oil spills had been recorded in Cook Inlet, 143 of which were proven to be industry spills. Jim then went on to document the importance of Kachemak Bay, which he called "*one of the world's most productive bays.*" In his conclusion Jim stated, "That the state issued oil leases for such a highly productive, intensely managed, valuable fisheries area—to say nothing about the tremendous scenic value—without local public hearings, in my opinion was a flagrant dereliction, and certainly an affront to the several thousand people who depend upon Kachemak Bay for their livelihood."

Bob Moss, a shrimp fisherman and former Board of Fish and Game Chairman, then presented testimony on the uniqueness of Kachemak Bay and his concern for damage possibilities from drilling or associated activities. In his conclusion, Bob said, "I believe the legislature should declare a two year moratorium on any drilling in this area, and with the period of time to be used researching and producing an environmental impact report. This should particularly include a complete marine inventory as well as detailed laboratory studies of the effects of hydrocarbons on shrimp and crab larvae by large spills or the long range effect of small build up spills."

The Senate Resources Committee took the concerns and recommendations from Smith, Rearden, Moss and others at the hearing to heart and soon there was action on several fronts. Senator Palmer termed the public hearing in

Homer the *"most productive hearing in my seven years in the legislature,"* and by early March had asked the oil companies involved to hold up exploratory drilling in Kachemak Bay. He said that six months to a year was needed to obtain basic information on the marine life in Kachemak Bay before drilling took place. He announced plans to introduce legislation to require environmental impact statements, and public hearings, before future lease sales. Palmer announced that the commissioner of Fish and Game had agreed to submit a proposal to the legislature that the Bluff Point area of Kachemak Bay be designated a "Critical Habitat Area."

The interesting and highly relevant conclusion from this initial hearing is that most of these recommendations and promises came to pass and that the future conduct of oil and gas leasing in Alaska was changed forever. Senators Palmer, Tillion, and others were able to get the initial legislation passed and obtain the funding to conduct a comprehensive marine study of Kachemak Bay (see Chapter 9). From a personal standpoint this was a big break at a much needed time in my career, since I was soon hired by the Habitat Division of ADF&G to head up the field portion of the Kachemak Bay environmental study.

Citizen's Battle On

The battle, which would eventually rage on for three years, had begun. From the citizen's standpoint I was assigned to work closely with Citizens for a Better Community and with a newly formed group called the Kachemak Bay Defense Fund. Frank Tupper was the director of the KBDF, and became one of the lead players in the Kachemak Bay buy-back effort. Strategy meetings were held and the two groups joined forces under the defense fund for most of the activities and actions that were to follow. There were many Homer fishermen and their wives, as well as other community members, who played key roles in a classic grass roots effort to save the bay.

Hearing on State and Corps of Engineers Drill Permits.

A hearing was held in Homer on May 18, 1974, with 120 persons in attendance. Shell Oil Company had applied for a permit to drill a well in Kachemak Bay and this hearing had a threefold purpose to hear testimony on (1) a state permit for exploratory drilling; (2) a proposed plan of operations; and (3) an offshore drilling permit required by the Army Corps of Engineers. Commercial fishing groups, citizens, and environmental groups testified with concerns for potential damage to fisheries resources and asked for a delay before proceeding with drilling. Shell Oil gave an hour-and-a-half presentation explaining how safe their operation would be and assuring residents that even if there was a spill there was nothing to worry about as oil in the water didn't really pose any threat to fisheries!

Colonel Charles A. Debelius, district engineer for Alaska, after hearing the public concern displayed at the hearing, decided to withhold a permit until an environmental impact statement (EIS) could be completed. The EIS process was completed by November 4 and on November 7 the Corps signed Shell's permit for exploratory drilling in Kachemak Bay.

Legal Action

The legal fight was now about to begin. In December 1974, a group of Homer area commercial fishermen and citizens filed a suit in superior court in Kenai asking that the state's oil lease sales of December, 1973, be set aside. The suit claimed the sale and subsequent leasing of tracts in the Kachemak Bay area were unconstitutional, because public notice of the sale was inadequate. The plaintiffs also claimed a lack of public hearings and studies to determine whether the sale was in the public interest.

Shortly after the lawsuit was filed, the Kachemak Bay Defense Fund asked for an injunction against exploratory drilling in Kachemak Bay until the court ruled on the legality of the oil and gas lease sale which had been held in December, 1973. When this injunction was turned down the KBDF appealed to the state supreme court. These actions bought time for fishermen and held up drilling by Shell throughout 1975.

Standard Oil Comes to Town

Standard Oil of California was next up with plans to drill in the area. Standard had been using the drill rig *George Ferris* on an exploratory well up the inlet off Cape Kasilof, and was now ready to drill for oil in Kachemak Bay. Standard had applied for a drilling permit and a hearing on the permit was held in Homer on January 29, 1975. Standard had witnessed the controversy surrounding Shell's permit and decided to bring the Big Oil guns to the little town of Homer. About 150 Homer residents showed up to greet the no less than eight SOCAL "experts." Homerites were about to receive the biggest snow job one could even imagine. Standard Oil testimony went on the entire morning with speaker after speaker attempting to calm and resolve all fears and concerns. Homer folks were told repeatedly that Standard Oil would take all possible steps to protect the environment and that the "best available technology" would be used. Meanwhile, their drill rig *George Ferris* was in dire trouble from its drilling exploits at Cape Kasilof where dynamite had to be used to free it from the drill site. In addition, a tug used on the project had been sunk causing a small oil spill. Homer citizens were aware of this as well of the rumor going around that the *Ferris* was an elderly rig which had been condemned in California!

Biologists and chemists for SOCAL gave a great dog-and-pony show with slides, graphs, and charts in an attempt to wow and influence the audience toward their basic position that there was "nothing to fear except fear itself." Slides of fish around platform legs in the Gulf of Mexico, slides of fish around natural oil seeps in California, statistics from oil company sponsored studies indicating that petroleum was not really harmful to fish or the environment. One of the big oil guns brought in from Chevron Oil Field Research Co. concluded that an offshore oil spill in Cook Inlet would have "insignificant effects." To say the least, Big O's presentation was *slick*!

Homer Speaks

During the question-and-answer period following the oil company presentations, Big Oil learned that Homer area residents were not as ignorant or naive as they may have presumed. Homer had already sat through much of the same malarkey during the previous hearings on the lease sale and Shell drill permit application. State Senator Clem Tillion bluntly told Standard that he didn't see any action from them that proposed drilling in Kachemak Bay "would be any cleaner than it had been anywhere else." Clem and other fishermen urged Standard to "stop comparing Cook Inlet's marine environment, tides, currents, and winds with waters in the Gulf of Mexico or anywhere else."

Homer residents and others then got a chance for their own presentations during the afternoon session. A total of 18 citizens testified and the next day the Homer News characterized this testimony as follows: "The research that had been done, the carefully worked speeches, the backgrounds and expertise of individuals, the heart-felt emotions expressed by people who really care about their environment and quality of life in Homer, Alaska—all were impressive. Several fishermen spoke, noting the importance of the commercial fishing industry to Homer, the unique biological richness of Kachemak Bay, and the loss of pots they have already suffered from increased surface traffic."

An ADF&G Assist

I personally took a great deal of pride in the overall quality of presentations by fishermen and other citizens of Homer who testified that day. Acting on

Commissioner Brooks' direction to "assist Citizens for a Better Community to the fullest," I had spent the previous week assembling information and assisting several of the would be witnesses with their presentations. By this time our habitat research team had been able to assemble even more information on the biological values of Kachemak Bay and the potential impacts from petroleum development and pollution. This information was made available to all who came to my office for assistance.

Perhaps the biggest impact of the day at the hearing had been made by a king crab. No one could forget when Bill Bledsoe, a giant of a man, came forward and deposited a huge crab on the table in front of Colonel Debelius and the hearing committee. "That's a king crab Colonel. His brothers and sisters and cousins are still out there in the bay. I know how they feel because I've been in touch with them." When Bledsoe finished his testimony, the Colonel eyed the mouth watering evidence and asked "Ah, Mr. Bledsoe, may I keep this crab?" Bledsoe replied "Hell no, I can get ten dollars for that!" He then snatched the crab off the table and promptly exited the room to a standing ovation.

An interesting side note and testimony to the politics of the times was that in contrast to the *Homer News* and *Anchorage Daily News,* both of which focused their coverage of the hearing on area resident concerns over oil development in Kachemak Bay; the *Anchorage Times* headline story of the hearing was titled "Bay Oil Poses No Threat."

Kachemak Bay Suit Dismissed

Homer area fishermen and residents lost their challenge to the legality of the 1973 state oil and gas lease sale in May 1975, when Superior Court Judge Shultz of Ketchikan ruled that it should be dismissed. His decision was based on the "doctrine of laches," which Shultz defined as "an unreasonable delay in asserting rights, which results in a disadvantage or prejudice to the defendants." Lawyer for the plaintiffs, Warren Matthews, then appealed the narrow legal ruling to the Alaska Supreme Court.

It was now time for newly elected Governor Jay Hammond to step up to the plate. He had campaigned the previous fall in support of the fishermen's cause and had expressed displeasure with the state's leasing policies that had led to the sale. Hammond had won the election by just 285 votes, and his support for fishermen had been credited by some as one of the reasons for his narrow victory. But ironically, during the campaign, actions of his chief advisor, Bob Palmer, may have inadvertently contributed to the late filing of the lawsuit. Palmer had, in Hammond's behalf, urged fishermen to delay filing their lawsuit, evidently to keep the issue alive for his campaign. Now was the time for Governor Hammond to match his actions with that of his heart. And he did so.

Governor Jay Joins the Battle

When campaigning for office in 1974, Hammond pledged to buy back the leases because of the potential danger to rich fisheries resources in the bay and because there was no public debate prior to the sale. It was not an easy decision. The governor's dilemma, according to his spokesman, Attorney General Avrum Gross, was that he had an "obligation to honor the state's written agreements," although he "personally felt heartsick" about the sale. Despite opposition within his own Republican party and the oil industry, he forged ahead.

By mid-June 1975, Governor Hammond announced his decision to side with fishermen in attempts to block exploratory drilling for oil in Kachemak Bay. Speaking for Hammond, Attorney General Avrum Gross said that the administration was considering asking the legislature to cancel the leases through state condemnation proceedings, and subsequently establish a sanctuary in the bay. The headline in a *New York Times* editorial on July 5, 1975 read "Alaska Governor Chooses Fish Over Oil in Kachemak Bay Fight."

Enter the Ferris

Meanwhile the jack-up drill rig *George Ferris* was making headlines again. The rig had been heavily damaged following a drilling operation off Cape Kasilof in January, when one of its leg jacks jammed and explosives were used to allow it to float free. Following this incident, the rig was to be towed to Kachemak Bay for repairs. Shell had promised to have a local fisherman aboard the rig when it was moved to guide it through the fishing grounds where several hundred crab pots, with buoys and lines, were in place. Inexplicably, the fisherman was never called and the rig was moved during the night and early morning hours, resulting in significant crab pot losses in the Bluff Point area. Knowing the sensitivity of the situation, Sun Marine Drilling, contractor for the rig, acted responsibly and quickly settled fishermen's claims for pot losses.

However, now the oil industry made a huge error which would eventually cost them the rights to ever drill in Kachemak Bay. They selected an area known as Mud Bay as the site to park the rig while repairs were underway. One would think the name alone would have brought about some concern and degree of caution. Fishermen cautioned that once a crab pot was mired in the mud in this area it was impossible to retrieve. Nonetheless, the four huge steel legs of the *Ferris* were lowered into the mud, eventually settling 82 feet deep.

Repairs to the rig took nearly five months and cost some $6 million. By early August, Offshore Constructors had begun conducting tests on the jacking system and shortly after the first rumors that the rig was stuck in the mud began to fly. The *Homer News* headline for August 28, 1975 read "Oil Rig Fouled In Rumors." When questioned by the media, Ralph Oxenrider, vice president of Offshore Contractors, stated that "there is no validity to the story

The jack-up oil drilling rig George Ferris. The portion of the four legs below deck are mired 82 feet deep in Mud Bay. Photo by Gary Williams

about our being stuck." The *Ferris* would then remain in Mud Bay for another eight months, manned with a skeleton crew and awaiting a final court decision, before it would make headlines again.

Citizens Battle On

On the citizen front it was the Kachemak Bay Defense Fund, led by the ever persistent Frank Tupper, that would organize the battle against the oil companies. Tupper joined forces with the North Pacific Fishermen's Association, headed up by Ken Moore, in a fund-raising effort to support the cause. By September 1975, the Defense Fund announced plans to launch a nationwide drive, mailing some 8,000 support flyers asking for contributions as well as sponsoring crab and shrimp feeds throughout the country. The fishermen's association donated seafood products for these fundraisers and helped the Defense Fund meet its legal bills, which had climbed to nearly $90,000. The donated product went to $10-a-plate crab feeds in Alaska and Outside and the rest of the money came in from the sale of T-shirts and donations from canneries, fishermen, and others. Tom Kizzia, in an article for the *Alaska Fisherman,* wrote "Aside from the attorneys there were few expenses: no Hilton Hotels (Tupper slept on couches when he traveled), no wining and dining, no legislators bought."

As the legal battle went on and as Governor Hammond and the legislature became more involved in the Kachemak Bay issue, a second group of Homer citizens, we'll call the "Boomers," decided it was time to get more actively involved. These folks were all good, well meaning, Homer citizens who simply held a different point of view. Many, of course were business people who stood to gain from oil development, should it come to the area. News coverage to this point in time, which included coverage of the three public hearings held in Homer, had indicated that the majority of Homer citizens was opposed to oil drilling in Kachemak Bay. The Boomers decided to try and demonstrate to legislators and others that this was somehow a false impression and that most people in Homer favored oil development. The way to do this, they decided, was through a somewhat cleverly designed and selectively distributed survey.

The Homer city manager and Homer mayor were very pleased with the poll results, as they seemed to indicate the opposite of what had been heard in public hearings. However, it soon became clear that the poll could not pass the "unbiased test." Many commercial fishermen and others known to have concerns, claimed that they had never been contacted and charged that the poll had been distributed selectively to people known to support oil development. The headline in the *Anchorage Times* read "Poll Taker Denies It Was Stacked" and in the *Homer News* "Homer Poll Results Unclear."

In any event, the mood and position of the vast majority of Homer citizens should have been clearly understood following a public meeting in February when Attorney General Avrum Gross was directed to seek clarification on how the people of Homer regarded the oil leases. When the oral testimonies were concluded Gross requested a show of hands by those who would support leaving the existing leases intact, allowing for the realistic prospects of oil drilling in Kachemak Bay. By the count of the attorney general, 18 persons of the approximately 400 in attendance, rose to the occasion. When the question was reversed, seeking condemnation of the leases, there was not enough time to count all who had risen. It was estimated that the ratio was 12-1 against development.

Governor Introduces Marine Sanctuary Bill

While Homer residents were duking it out in a classic public relations battle, Attorney General Gross, under a directive from Governor Hammond, was back in Juneau drafting a bill that would create a Marine Sanctuary in Kachemak Bay and condemn the oil leases there. Shortly after introduction to the House Resources Committee in early March, the bill was promptly tabled on a motion by Homer representative Leo Rhode. Leo had told committee members two public opinion polls conducted in his district showed residents were "opposed overwhelmingly" to Hammond's plan for a marine sanctuary in the bay.

It was now time for some damage control. Fortunately, preliminary results had just become available from two environmental studies that had been initiated at the beginning of the Kachemak Bay debacle. One was ADF&G's own study on the "Impact of Oil on the Kachemak Bay Environment," for which I had been assigned the position of field project leader. The other was a study on the potential impacts of oil on the marine environment by the National Marine Fisheries Service. Bob Palmer, Hammond's chief lieutenant, was determined to see that the House Resources Committee hold hearings on these reports.

House Resources Hearing

As field project leader for the Kachemak Bay marine studies, I was called down to Juneau to give a report on our findings. Certain committee members who were considered pro-oil got wind of the nature of the report I was scheduled to give and knew it would not be good for their cause. House Resources Chairman decided to delay my testimony and refused to schedule it on the committee agenda. After two days of delay pressure was brought about by both Palmer and Senate Resource Chairman Chancy Croft to have the committee hear the report. I had gone down to Juneau on short notice and on arrival didn't have much of a formal report prepared. The two-day delay gave me time to organize the information I had brought with me and to prepare several visual aids in the form of transparencies. Besides this, I was mad when Croft had told me that the committee was purposely holding me off in the hopes that I would return to Homer without giving the report!

By the time my report was finally scheduled, a great deal of interest had developed over the proceedings in the House Resources Committee. The meeting room was jam-packed with senators and representatives from other committees as well as the press and a few citizens from the Kachemak Bay area. I ended up taking more than an hour of their precious time with a 24-page report. When I was finished, they had seen documentation showing that Kachemak Bay was in fact one of the "most highly productive marine environments in the world," how the current gyres in outer Kachemak Bay allowed larval stages of crab and shrimp to develop and settle within the bay, that recently concluded bioassay studies indicated that these larvae were extremely sensitive to very low levels of hydrocarbons, and finally, that the leases that had been issued were smack in the middle of the most biologically sensitive area. From the questioning that went on for the next half hour, I could sense that I had raised some awareness among committee members.

The next biologist to speak to the committee was Stanley "Jeep" Rice from the National Marine Fisheries Service. Rice reported that his scientific study showed that petroleum development in shellfish-rich Kachemak Bay "poses a higher environmental risk than in most other areas of Alaska." Rice said that because of the whirlpool action of the current, strong tides and wind in Kachemak Bay, "there is a higher potential for poisoning of marine life."

Big Oil Guns Speak

The game continued and now it was time for damage control by committee members opposed to the bill. So they called in oil industry experts to try and offset the damage perceived to have been done by the reports Jeep and I had given. It was truly a classic, unbelievable performance that only the most gullible pro-oil advocate would buy. On April 11, 1976 the *Anchorage Times* reported this testimony under the headline "Industry, Fishermen Want Kachemak Oil." The *Times* quoted Clayton McAuliffe, senior research associate with Chevron Oil Field Research Company, as follows: "It would not be possible to spill enough oil in Kachemak Bay to significantly affect fin fish and shellfish. It would take 200 million barrels of crude oil to provide one part per million (PPM) water-soluble fraction in Kachemak Bay. This would require the complete loss of all oil from 95 tankers of 300,000 ton capacity to achieve this amount."

Three other spokesmen for Shell Oil went on to testify to the effect that fisheries and oil operations were completely compatible in Kachemak Bay and that there was really no realistic threat to the bay from an oil spill.

The oil companies had done their job and now committee members had the justification they sought to water down the Senate version of the Marine Sanctuary bill. They added an amendment to the bill to allow exploratory drilling to go on in Kachemak Bay while negotiations proceeded. No doubt this was a big blow to the fishermen and citizens who were fighting the lease sale, but it would not be long before the tide turned in their favor.

The Tide Turns

The stage was set for the final act of the *George Ferris*. The *Ferris* had been at center stage before—in fact, at one time in a major Hollywood production. In 1971, the *Ferris* had been cast as the secret headquarters for an international crime syndicate in the James Bond film *Diamonds Are Forever*. As jet fighters strafed the machine gun nests placed on the deck of the *Ferris*, Bond "blew the *Ferris* into the sky" at the climax of the film. This time the *Ferris* was to change the outcome of the Kachemak Bay oil lease battle and the history of Homer and the bay forever.

The *Ferris* had been sitting in Mud Bay for nearly a year following extensive repairs made after the Cape Kasilof incident. In early May the rumors of the previous summer, that the *Ferris* was "stuck in the mud," proved to be true. The trouble started when the rig was getting ready to leave Kachemak Bay for a job further up in Cook Inlet. The barge had been jacked down into the water at low tide and legs pinned in place in hopes that the incoming tide would create enough pressure and buoyancy to suck the legs free from the 82 feet of mud. Didn't work. The legs of the rig buckled under pressure when the mud wouldn't give and the incoming tide swamped the rig.

An oil spill from the flooded diesel tanks on the deck of the *Ferris* eventually resulted and efforts to contain the spill, even under ideal conditions, were unsuccessful. Newspaper headlines at the time read "Drill Rig Stuck to Bottom of Kachemak Bay," "Oil Spill in Kachemak Bay," and "ADF&G: Nothing is working in Kachemak Bay." Following the incident, Ralph Oxenrider, vice president for Offshore Contractors in charge of the rig at the time, was interviewed by the *Homer News* and stated "We've had trouble with that damn thing ever since Sean Connery blew it up." The *Ferris* was to be "blown up" one final time when in late June explosive charges were used to free it from the mud of Mud Bay.

Legislature Acts Quickly

Within two days of the *Ferris* incident the legislature in Juneau was in action on the Marine Sanctuary Bill. The House Resources Committee had amended the bill and strengthened it to include everything Governor Hammond had wanted including a moratorium on drilling, authority to negotiate a buy back agreement, and allow condemnation of the leases if a buyback agreement could not be reached. Present at the final hearing on the bill were Tupper and Phil Daniels from the United Fishermen of Alaska; but there were no oil company representatives in sight. The bill passed the House on a 26-13 vote and shortly after passed the Senate on a unanimous voice vote. Hammond then signed the bill. Near the end of the session a final crab feed was held in Juneau by the Kachemak Bay Defense Fund and among the some 370 attendees were Governor Jay Hammond and Natural Resource Commissioner Guy Martin. Hammond was said to have dubbed the event the "George Ferris Memorial Dinner."

Kachemak Bay Leases Repurchased

It was obvious at this point that this case was making history. Nothing like this had ever happened before. Big Oil had lost a battle with fishermen and other concerned citizens of the Kachemak Bay area. And the state was involved in buying back oil leases it had sold in 1973 for $25 million. There was the threat, no promise, of condemnation if oil companies did not come to the table to negotiate the buyback. All of this was not only big news in Alaska but outside media including the *Wall Street Journal, New York Times, and Science Magazine* had covered the story. Hammond and Attorney General Gross went right to work negotiating with the oil companies. By early January the state had reached agreement with SOCAL, then in February with Texaco. Shell Oil held out until the very end and finally came to agreement as the deadline approached.

The total cost of the repurchase was $28.4 million, costing the state about $3.5 million. Gross said, "If Kachemak Bay is really saved I think we've done something valuable." Reflecting on the fishermen's victory later, he commented, "All the people of Homer had to do was turn around the entire oil industry and the government of the state. And, incredibly, they did it." Governor Hammond said the repurchase "represents a major turning point in Alaska's history. It represents the end of an era when we sold our oil resources without any real reflection on the impact from the sale, simply for the purpose of gaining immediate revenue to run our government."

Postscript on Oil Exploration

At the very time that the battle for Kachemak Bay had been won, another battle, this one over Lower Cook Inlet, had just begun. This fight, because it was a federal government Outer Continental Shelf (OCS) sale, and because it was outside the confines of Kachemak Bay, took on a different tone. Besides, by the end of the Kachemak Bay saga, most fishermen were pretty well burned out and not quite ready to take on another big battle. Even so there were a few, led again by the ever determined Tupper (now known as "Mad Dog"), who were ready and willing to engage.

The sale, which was originally scheduled for January 1977, was to offer nearly 900,000 acres of Lower Cook Inlet. The sale included some sensitive areas off English Bay and in the immediate vicinity of the Bluff Point Sanctuary. Although Hammond did not oppose this sale, he did ask for certain tracts to be deleted. A coalition of Natives, environmentalists, and fishermen then filed suit to delay the sale, which had been rescheduled for late February. An injunction was issued and the sale was held up pending a review and decision by Secretary of the Interior Cecil Andrus.

May 1977 Washington D.C. meeting with Secretary of Interior Cecil Andrus regarding Cook Inlet Oil Leasing. L. to R: Loren Flagg, Frank Tupper, Charles Koningsberg, Andrus, Bill Bledsoe, and Paul Jones. Department of Interior Photo

The Kachemak Bay Defense Fund decided to send a contingent to Washington, DC to meet and lobby Andrus to either cancel the sale or at least delete some of the more sensitive tracts. I was asked to join the group and received permission from my supervisors to do so. In early May our group of five—Frank Tupper, Paul Jones, Bill Bledsoe, Charles Koningsberg, and me—met for nearly two hours with Secretary Andrus in a meeting that was originally scheduled for 30 minutes. We were able to supply Andrus with facts about the fisheries resources of Lower Cook Inlet, including the size of commercial catch, critical habitat areas, and the biology of the area. He seemed extremely interested and asked a lot of questions. At one point one of his staff interrupted him to remind him that he had another appointment for which he was already 30 minutes late. Andrus replied "Those big oil wigs can wait, these guys are a lot more interesting!"

We came away with the impression that Andrus was strongly considering further deletion of tracts from the lease sale area, particularly those off Anchor Point. When the sale was finally held in late October 1977, several tracts totaling about 200,000 acres had been deleted and additional environmental protections had been added to sale provisions. All in all, we believed our trip to Washington, DC had been worthwhile.

Chapter 11
A Sportsman's Paradise

Land's End

I worked in Homer for ADF&G from 1968 to 1979. And of course, it was not all work. I was stationed in a virtual sportsman's paradise considering what the biologically diverse Kachemak Bay area and nearby Anchor River had to offer. My first sportfishing experience in Alaska was casting off the end of the Homer Spit for Dolly Varden trout, which were in some years available by late April. One time my son, Mitch, I think about seven at the time, caught a decent-sized Dolly at the end of the Spit behind the restaurant at Land's End. Earl Hillstrand, a legislator and owner of Land's End at the time, observed Mitch hauling in the big Dolly from the restaurant window and proceeded to announce this event over his loudspeaker system to all who were having lunch at the time. "Look out back folks, a young lad is just now hauling in a big fish!," Earl bellowed out. Soon his patrons were all glued to the windows and applause rang out when the

My son, Mitch, with one of his first Dolly Varden trout, caught behind Land's End, at the end of the Homer Spit.

fish was finally landed. I think Earl got a big kick out of doing this sort of thing for his clientele; and as a proud father, so did I!

Fishing the Anchor

The Anchor River was about 15 miles up the road from Homer and offered excellent fishing for several species of fish including king and coho salmon, steelhead, and Dolly Varden trout. I caught my first king salmon on the Anchor River in late May 1968 and continued to fish the river for kings in May and early June during the years I was stationed in Homer. The Anchor was a fun river to fish for kings, especially once you hooked into a big one. Once hooked they often ran downstream and if you couldn't go with them, you would end up losing the fight. There are a lot of stories, mostly hilarious, surrounding some of these great battles and someday someone will probably write a book chronicling a few of the more renowned fights. I'll just relate one.

The Anchor River can produce some nice sized kings. This one, taken by the author in 1971, weighed in at 35 pounds.

Sam Miller was one of my fishing and hunting buddies during the time we were in Homer. One year Sam was fishing the river on opening day when the typical opening day crowds were on the river. He wasn't able to squeeze into a very fishable location but managed to find a spot along a brushy bank just above the "Slide Hole," one of the best fishing holes on the river. Sam hooked into a big king salmon and as the fish headed downstream his choices were limited as there was no bank to work along and the river was too fast and deep for him to wade into and follow the fish. Sam was never one to give up easily on anything and, not about to let this fish go. With his chest waders pulled up high he entered the river, leaned back, and holding tightly onto his rod proceeded to float down through the Slide Hole following the fish downstream. As he floated past the throngs of fishermen along the banks, who were by this time cheering him on, Sam, with a big, and somewhat sheepish smile on his face, yelled out "Playing through!"

Oil in the Anchor

I caught my first-ever steelhead and trapped my first Alaska mink on the Anchor River and learned to love this river much as I had loved the Elmwood River, where I had spent all my early years. Thus I was pretty upset one day in early March, 1970, when trapper Ed Schollenberg came into my office with a beaver he had caught in the river that was covered with oil. Homer Wildlife Protection officer Ed Martin and I investigated and discovered that Standard Oil was drilling an exploratory well on Chakok Creek, a tributary to the Anchor. They had dug a small drainage ditch from their sump pond, which was full of oily wastes, directly to Chakok Creek. Unbelievably, they were intentionally allowing oil to flow freely into the river! We informed the workers at the site to block off the ditch, then took some photos, river water samples, and sump pond samples for evidence. The oil flow into the river was soon stopped and Standard was eventually fined $5,000 by the state for their folly. The arrogance and carelessness of this act, along with all the many oil spills I had observed on my flights over the inlet, left me with a bad early impression of the Cook Inlet oil industry.

I wrote a poem that was published under my "Trapper Joe" byline in the *Homer News* shortly after this incident, but I can recall only the first few lines:

> *Way down on the Kenai, not too many moons ago,*
> *Was a river called the Anchor, and how I loved it so.*
> *In the spring I fished for kings, when they came for nature's call,*
> *And in the summer for the silvers; then the steelhead in the fall.*
> *And then one day ....*

The rest of the poem basically described the threat posed to this river by oil spills, other pollutants, and uncontrolled development. Fortunately, the Anchor River has withstood the stresses of time and is still in pretty good shape today. Fortunately also, because of stronger regulations and more stringent fines, the oil industry has cleaned up its act somewhat and incidents like the Anchor River spill are less frequent today.

Fishing Around Kachemak Bay

The seafood bounty and sporting opportunities around Kachemak Bay in the late '60s and throughout the '70s could only be described as fantastic. Salmon of five species were available at many locations around the bay. All five species were known by two common names: pinks (humpies), chums (dogs), reds (sockeye), kings (chinook), and silvers (cohos) and could all be harvested by rod and reel within their respective seasons.

The species I fished for most within the bay were pinks and silvers. Pinks could be caught from shore off the end of the Homer Spit and within nearly all the inlets on the south side of the bay. When "ocean-bright," pink salmon are a quality fish, both from a sportfishing and dinner table standpoint. The problem with pinks is that once they are exposed to freshwater near stream mouths, they turn dark and soft fleshed rapidly. The trick is to catch them before this transformation occurs. This could be done in places like China Poot Bay and Tutka Bay Lagoon, but timing was critical. My favorite place to take visiting friends and relatives was Tutka Bay Lagoon, where you could cast and catch pink salmon until your arms ached. As the pink run progressed there was usually a lot of culling involved to obtain a few quality fish.

For silvers, my favorite fishing hole was Mud Bay, where casting hardware from shore at high tide was the preferred technique. Silvers could also be taken near or in some of the streams across the bay, usually in late August or September. Two of the most productive spots that I ever fished were Clearwater Slough (a tributary to Fox River) and Rocky River along the outer coast on the Gulf of Alaska side.

Fox River

One of my fishery biologist cohorts, Ken Roberson, and I made a trip by canoe up the Fox River to Clearwater Slough in mid-September for both business and pleasure. The business part was to try and recover tags from silvers that we had tagged in salt water during August as they passed through Mud Bay. The pleasure part was the method we had decided to use for recovery—rod and reel, of course! Silvers were schooled up at the mouth of Clearwater Slough and we caught fish on virtually every cast. We did this for two days and it is still probably the best silver salmon fishing I've ever experienced. And yes, to justify our trip as business, we did recapture several tagged silvers.

Rocky River

My good friend Tony Neal had a Kachemak Bay boat, the *Beaver II*. On a couple of occasions Tony, my son Mitch, and I took it across the bay to Jakalof Bay where we docked the boat and then traveled several miles in a borrowed four-wheel-drive vehicle over a logging road to Rocky River. This river supported a good run of silvers and some of the biggest Dolly Varden trout on the southern Kenai Peninsula. For combination fishing—silver salmon and Dolly Varden—this river was hard to beat. On one of our trips we discovered several large trees right along the stream bank that had been recently felled by loggers. A few were actually in the stream! Since there was a 50 foot buffer zone in effect for logging on this stream, these felled trees were evidence of a clear and flagrant violation. So again I was in a position to combine work with what was supposed to be a pleasure trip. I took pictures for evidence and soon after this practice was halted and the timber company fined. Another industry—another folly!

Halibut Galore

Kachemak Bay was renowned for good halibut fishing, but until you've had the experience, it's hard to imagine just what "good" means. Over the years I fished halibut from several boats with several friends in Kachemak Bay and can't remember getting skunked too often. Maybe on a bad-weather day

Mitch, his aunt Susan Flagg Poole, and our Kachemak Bay boat, the Beaver ll.

when you couldn't get out to one of your favorite holes. It was very common to limit out on halibut in the 20-to-40 pound class in the 1970s, and luckily still is today—although now you might have to run a few more miles out of the bay to find a good hole. It was not rare at all to catch a fish or two in the 50-to-90 pound class, and on occasion a fish more than 100 pounds was landed. Sometimes the fishing was "hot and heavy" and a boat limit could be taken in just a matter of minutes at the right stage of the tide.

Bigger halibut are usually shot before being brought aboard with anything ranging from a .22 caliber rifle or pistol to a .410 shotgun. On one occasion my wife, Sandra, and I were out in the "60-Foot Hole" with a friend from Fish and Game. He taught gun safety and was one of the most cautious persons around guns that I had ever known. He had never caught a big halibut and when he hooked into one he got a little overly excited when he brought it up to the side of the boat. I was about to dispatch his big halibut for him with my .25 caliber Colt revolver when, evidently worried that I might hit the line or hook, he yelled out, "No, no—don't shoot him until we get him in the boat!" Not too good a practice in a big boat, let alone the 20-footer we were in! He was able to laugh this off after the trip, but for obvious reasons I have not used his name here.

Shellfish Heaven

Kachemak Bay was chock- full of crab, shrimp, and clams during the years we lived in Homer. You were allowed to fish crab or shrimp pots for "personal use" and this could be actually done for a while within the boat harbor or off the end of the Homer dock if you didn't have access to a boat. I caught my first Dungeness crab from a hand-pulled pot inside the small boat harbor before the big harbor expansion took place in the early '70s. King crab and shrimp could be caught with small pots or nets off the main dock. Our first clamming adventures were out along the northeast side of the Homer Spit where at low tide we would join in with several other Homer families in the pursuit of cockles. They were so abundant at the time that digging was not required to obtain your limit since there were ample numbers of cockles just lying above the surface of the mud.

Having access to a "bay boat" opened up a whole new world to the would-be shell-fisherman. Nearly all the bays on the south side had clam beaches, where cockles, littlenecks, butter clams, and several other species of clams were harvested. Our favorite spots were McDonald Spit, Sadie Cove, and Tutka Bay. We often carried one or two "dungy pots" along on a clam expedition and let these fish while we were off digging a limit of steamers. At the end of the day we would have quite a feast of steamed clams, Dungeness crab, and maybe a salmon or halibut if we were lucky enough to catch one after the clam tide. Not quite a New England Clambake, but pretty darn close!

Back-Breaking Work

King and tanner crab were another challenge for the sport or personal-use fisherman. They required bigger, heavier pots and were usually found at greater depths than the smaller Dungeness crab. Guys with bigger boats supporting davits and pot pullers had no problem accessing these critters but those without such mechanical or hydraulic devices had a much harder time. Most guys would not even think of trying to lift a commercial-size king crab pot from great depths, let alone from the shallows. But not my buddy Nick Dudiak. When it came to work or pursuit of fish and game, Nick never did anything in a small way. Nick was strong as an ox and not about to be stopped by the fact that his boat wasn't equipped to pull the larger pots.

Nick went out and bought a 6-by-6 foot crab pot that had to weigh a couple hundred pounds and set it out about a mile above the Homer Spit. This was in the late '70s when the crab were running big, and he may not have factored that into his thinking. When he tried to retrieve it off the bottom the next day he could barely budge it, but reasoned that since he had moved it a little by himself that two guys could probably pull it in. That's when I got the call to help. Luckily I brought my wife, Sandra, along and Nick had his wife, Norma, aboard when it came time to start pulling. Nick and I had barely got the crab- laden pot started off the bottom when we both cried out for help. The wives joined in and about 10 minutes later, and after frequent rests, we had hand-pulled the pot into the boat. I had been out on many commercial crab boats and had seen a lot of pots come up full, but never anything like this! The pot was not just full, but full of the largest king crab I had seen in my dozen years of working in lower Cook Inlet. With an average size of more than 10 pounds, it was no wonder we had literally broken our backs to retrieve this pot. Family and friends were well fed for a while! Nick, Norma, and Sandra would all go on to have back problems later in their lives. Since I never developed a back problem Nick used one of his favorite expressions on me whenever we recalled the event in future years: "Loren, you must have been *shamming*."

Bay of Abundance

When you think about it—five species of Pacific salmon, three species of trout, (including steelhead), Pacific halibut, three species of crab, shrimp, rockfish (and other bottom fish) and several species of clams—all available in the Kachemak Bay area. It is easy then to make the argument that Homer, and other lower Kenai Peninsula area residents, live in a true sportsmen's paradise. And I didn't even mention the hunting and many other outdoor activities to be experienced in the area! That is one reason why, when the time came to make a move up the highway to Soldotna, my family and I did so with some regret.

Chapter 12
Oceans to Rivers

Moving up the Highway

Following a few somewhat slim statewide salmon fishing seasons in the early 1970s, a new division of ADF&G was created by the legislature called the "Fisheries Rehabilitation Enhancement and Development Division," FRED for short. The Kachemak Bay marine study had been completed, the Habitat Division had decided to centralize their personnel in Anchorage, and I was a part of that plan. Not wanting to live or work out of Anchorage, I looked for work elsewhere and was lucky to find a Fisheries Biologist lll opening with the FRED Division 75 miles up the road in Soldotna. By this time both Laurie and Mitch were off to college so it was just Sandra and me left to make the move. We did so in the fall of 1979.

Working for the FRED Division still allowed me to do fisheries research; however this time it was to be in the freshwater, rather than the marine environment. The two main drainages I was assigned to study were the Kenai and Kasilof River systems. I had two very capable Fishery Biologist ll's as assistants—Gary Kyle and Dave Waite—and that made my job during the next eight years an enjoyable one. We were also blessed to have extremely capable "seasonal" fishery technicians on our team and a few—including Dave Litchfield, Gary Todd, Terry Tobias, and Pat Shields—stayed with me for several years and eventually went on to land permanent jobs with the state.

Rehab & Enhance

Our job with FRED was to develop programs within the central Kenai Peninsula area aimed at rehabilitating and enhancing salmon stocks. Some projects were already underway at the time I came on board and one of my main assignments was to design and implement field research studies to evaluate these projects. The program included the Crooked Creek Hatchery (located at Kasilof), which supported a sockeye salmon fry- stocking project at Tustumena Lake and a king salmon smolt stocking project at Crooked Creek. FRED had also initiated plans for construction of a new hatchery at Trail Lakes near Moose Pass, which would eventually support several salmon-stocking projects on both the central and lower Kenai Peninsula.

Crooked Creek

We had a salmon weir on Crooked Creek and conducted a creel survey at the confluence of Crooked Creek and the Kasilof River to evaluate the king salmon return. The weir also served as the king salmon egg take site. To evaluate the sockeye smolt outmigration from Tustumena Lake, we constructed huge aluminum smolt traps to intercept and estimate the survival of these fish.

Hidden Lake

At Hidden Lake we took water chemistry and plankton samples to determine the lake's potential for sockeye salmon smolt production. The lake was eventually stocked with sockeye fry from the Trail Lakes Hatchery and a smolt trap and adult salmon weir were constructed to assess survival and ultimate success of this program.

Quartz Creek

One of our most challenging projects was constructing an adult salmon weir on Quartz Creek, a tributary to Kenai Lake. Quartz Creek was deep and fast and we had our hands full trying to maintain a weir in place. A few biologists, including yours truly, and technicians experienced some very cold dunks into the icy waters of Quartz Creek during this project! We didn't end up using Quartz Creek as an enhancement site, but did add a great deal of information on the size and timing of the king, sockeye, and coho runs that utilize this system for spawning. In addition to adults, we also conducted extensive research on juvenile salmon using the system for rearing. It turned out that the Quartz Creek system, which includes Crescent Creek, Dave's Creek, and Tern Lake, was much more important for salmon spawning and rearing than previously thought.

Kenai Kings

We cooperated on a couple of different studies under a program funded by the U.S. Fish and Wildlife Service (USFWS) and directed by Carl Burger, a senior fisheries biologist for that agency. The first project I participated in was the capture and tagging of king salmon in the lower Kenai River in the early '80s. This study was conducted to determine run timing and distribution of king salmon within the river system. Fish were captured by floating a small gill net at different locations until a king salmon was "hit." The fish were brought alongside the boat and released into a live box where they could be sampled for age, weight, and length (AWL) and then fitted with two different tags. One of the tags was a radio tag which would submit a distinct signal for each individual fish so that they could be tracked as they moved up the Kenai River and into different spawning areas.

One of the early capture areas was in the vicinity of the "Pillars," a popular fishing hole in the lower river. I was assisting with the project one day when an interesting, and eye opening, event occurred. We had captured an average-sized Kenai king—pushing 40 pounds—and after extracting this fish from the net, collecting the AWL information, and attaching a couple of tags, had released it alongside the island directly across from the Pillars boat ramp. While still in the process of recording the data from this fish we noted that a fishing boat just above us had hooked up with a king. We motored out of the way and got set up to do our next drift with the net. Pretty soon the fisherman who had hooked the king pulled alongside to show off his catch. Darned if it didn't have a radio tag attached, and sure enough it was the one we had just released! This fish had taken the bait within just two or three minutes of being released and as a result didn't provide much in the way of biological data, just an interesting side note.

Benjamin Creek

Later that season, when it came time to try and recapture a few tags from the spawning grounds, I flew into Benjamin Creek—a tributary to the Killey River—with USFWS personnel. As we followed radio-tagged fish, it had become clear that the Killey was by far the most important spawning area for early run king salmon, and thus additional work was to be focused there. We camped on Benjamin Creek for a couple of nights and worked on recapturing tagged kings during the day. It was difficult to sleep at night, since several brown bears were heard parading through camp and splashing around in the creek nearby in pursuit of the same fish that we were after. In the morning we tried to scare the remaining bears off so we could get to work capturing the tagged kings, utilizing both nets and fishing rods. There were some big kings in Benjamin Creek, a few pushing 70 pounds, so the capture phase of this project proved to be quite exciting. We were all soaking wet and covered with fish slime by the end of the day.

Retirement Beckons

By the late 1980s ADF&G was starting to experience large budget cuts by the legislature, which was in turn responding to a decrease in state revenues due to declining oil production. As the newest division within ADF&G, the FRED Division was taking the largest hits to their budget and it wouldn't be long until the division was eliminated. With the handwriting on the wall, and not wanting to move again, I decided to take advantage of another legislative action designed to improve the budget situation—this one called "early retirement." There were some significant perks to the early retirement offer, the biggest being an offer of three additional years of retirement credit to your account should you choose the program. It was an easy decision for me, especially since I had another endeavor in mind—this time as a Kenai River sportfishing guide.

Chapter 13
Guiding on the Kenai River

Learning the River

When we moved up from Homer in 1979 we had built a new home on the Kenai River at River Mile 22, just above the Soldotna Bridge. By the summer of 1980, I had purchased an 18-foot Monarch riverboat and started fishing the river pretty regularly. While I knew the lower river below the bridge pretty well from my fish and game work in the late '60s-early '70s, I wasn't familiar with the middle portion of the river above our house. I knew that it was faster, shallower, and had far more rocks but I was anxious to learn how to run it and to find out where the best fishing holes were. Thankfully, one of the fisheries technicians I had hired to work with the FRED Division had done some fishing on this stretch of the river and offered to help me out. Aaron Horwath turned out to be very knowledgeable on this section of the river and I was soon catching king salmon in various holes for several miles above my house. This knowledge came in handy when I later became a guide.

I didn't learn everything about the middle river right away. Lots of props were taken out on rocks and sandbars as well as a couple of lower units during the first two or three years. But the most serious, and funniest (in retrospect) thing that happened while trying to learn the middle river was slicing a hole in the bottom of the boat and nearly sinking while I was trying to make it back to my dock.

Swamped!

In the early '80s I was still doing a lot of drift fishing, as opposed to back trolling, in both the lower and middle rivers. I was in a drift from Swiftwater

Lucky Ladies

(above) This picture of daughter Laurie donned the cover of Flaggs Kenai Charters fishing brochure. Photo by Mitch Flagg

(upper right) Family friend Kelley Miller with her first Kenai River salmon.

(right) Friend and neighbor Lisa Meloon shows how to pose for a picture if you want your king to look as big as it should.

(right) A gorgeous day on the Kenai River near Eagle Rock. Stacie Mallette and Laurie display two beautiful king salmon in the 40-to-50 pound class.

(lower left) Sandra with her biggest king ever, a 69 pound hen taken off the tail end of "Snafu Island" in 1986.

(lower right) Alaskan, Super Cub pilot, Gwen Ferrari displays her 55 pound king salmon caught in the lower Kenai River off "Snafu Island," July 1989.

to Soldotna Creek with Sandra, Allen Quimby and his wife, and their son Shane when I spotted a patch of whitewater just ahead of our line of drift. Thinking that the rock below the surface was deep enough to just float over I didn't bother to make a course correction. Well, I guess that I hadn't figured on the amount of weight we had aboard—four adults and a teenager crammed into my 18-foot flat-bottom, and thin-skinned riverboat. As we drifted over the rock we heard a scraping noise and soon river water gushed into the boat. My dock was a little less than a quarter mile below so I decided to make a run for it despite cries of panic from my crew. When we pulled in to the dock the boat swamped to nearly the gunnels. As we climbed out, soaked to the gills, everyone had a pretty good laugh at my expense!

The nice thing about aluminum is that it's relatively easy to fix. My good friend and Crooked Creek hatchery manager Bob Och, an excellent welder, had me back in the water within two days. I had learned a basic lesson of power-boat river navigation and was never to repeat this mistake—avoid any and all whitewater and the rocks below!

Show Me the River

Living on the river and having a riverboat tied up behind the house led to the beginnings of my guide career. When Fish and Game bosses or personnel from other cooperating agencies came to town and wanted to "see the river,"—I was the go-to guy. Since "see the river," also meant "let's go fishing," I obtained a lot of early guiding experience, usually at the price of a six-pack and a tank of gas. Of course the six-pack was never indulged in (at least by me) until we made it back to the dock and were (hopefully) hanging up our fish for pictures. I made several trips ranging from the Naptown Rapids down to the cannery docks near the mouth of the river during this time period in an effort to *show* "visiting dignitaries" the Kenai River.

Becoming a Registered Guide

While working for ADF&G I was not allowed to be a registered guide on the Kenai and thus could not receive compensation for taking people fishing. By 1987 there was a lot of talk about the need to limit the number of guides, who were by this time being permitted and regulated by the Alaska Division of Parks. I was concerned that if I did not get registered fairly soon that I could get shut out of the process. So when I decided to accept the early-retirement offer from the state in May, 1987, the first thing I did was register as a Kenai River guide at Alaska State Parks.

First Guide Trip

Now officially a guide, I was scheduled to conduct my first trip in early June, when in late May I got a call from good friend and Deep Creek guide Mike Chihuly. He had a good friend and longtime client, Phil Todd, who was trying to show some fellow workers from General Electric what fishing was all about in Alaska. They had gotten "blown off" from Deep Creek fishing that day and were desperate to get out fishing somewhere. The Kenai River was still low and I hadn't even done a "shake-down" trip yet so I was a little reluctant to take this group, but Mike prevailed. After Phil and his group arrived, we loaded up in my Jeep and trailered the boat down to Stewart's Landing, where we launched into a river that was not just low, but was so muddied up you couldn't see even an inch or two into the river. We proceeded to hit a few sandbars, took out one prop, and dinged up another pretty good. And we proceeded to get skunked!

I wasn't used to this, and this was not how I wanted to start off my Kenai River guide career! I felt pretty foolish and incompetent and there was a grim silence as we rode back in the Jeep. I had made up my mind that I wasn't going to take any money from Phil and his party, but somehow even that didn't help the way I was feeling. Then, on impulse, as we crossed the Soldotna Bridge I spoke up "How about we stop here at the Nightwatch (bar and grill) and I buy you guys a beer?" After a couple of brews Phil noted how they really wanted to fish Deep Creek the next day, but that Mike was booked up. I called Mike for them but he said that everyone he knew was booked up since they were near the peak of the king salmon run. I related this to Phil and he said, "Well Loren, could you possibly take us?" I had fished Deep Creek from the 18-foot Bay Runner that I had at the time, but had never guided down there. And I wasn't really set up with the proper gear for the combo king salmon/-halibut trip that most guides offered in this saltwater fishery. I explained this to Phil, but he prevailed and said, "we'll make it work."

Guiding at Deep Creek

I spent the next couple of hours rounding up some extra halibut poles, a Deep Creek anchor, and some bait. We set off early the next morning and proceeded to have a great trip, limiting out on halibut and catching more than our share of king salmon that day. Mike was impressed enough to hire me as an early-season backup guide at Deep Creek for the next few years and Phil became a good friend and client who ended up fishing with me just about every year for the next 15 years. I learned a lesson there that I applied throughout my guide career as well as my life: If you treat people right, good

Kenai Kids

(above)Kids love to catch cohos. L. to R: Eric Kempf, Russell Dukowitz, Vanessa Dukowitz, and Lee Kempf.

Lee's friend Collin Moore shows his 45 pound hen taken in the lower Kenai River Satellite Hole. July 22, 2007.

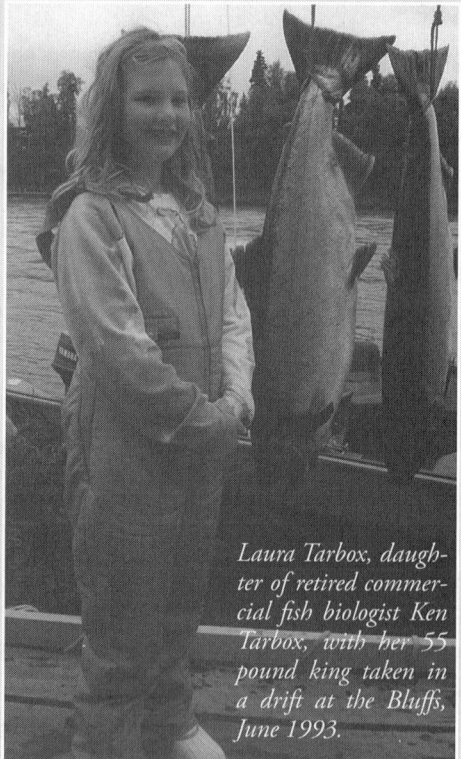

Laura Tarbox, daughter of retired commercial fish biologist Ken Tarbox, with her 55 pound king taken in a drift at the Bluffs, June 1993.

(right) Michael Hill, son of my former Kenai River guide partner Rich Hill, and Lee Kempf, with three silver bright cohos.

(left) Alaska gals love to fish too. Vanessa Dukowitz with a silver she was able to "rib" the boys about.

(right) Gramps is about to release a small salmon for Eric Kempf. Eric wanted to be able to keep fishing for a bigger one!

things will happen. After that first guided trip on the Kenai, whenever I had a disappointing trip on the river that might possibly be due to my performance as a guide, I would give clients a choice between another trip for free on the river, or their money back. In 20 years of guiding I only ended up returning money one time.

Client Becomes Lifelong Friend

I was into just my second week of my first year of guiding when I met another client, Frank Lamberti from New York, who would become a life-long friend. Meeting people like Frank and his wife Lea, I was finding out, was one of the most enjoyable parts of guiding. Frank had been sent my way by Terry Holliday, a big-game guide, spotter pilot, and acquaintance of my son, Mitch. As a sportsman who had hunted pretty much all over the world, Frank and I hit it off right away. Our friendship, and mutual respect, was sealed the day after his wife had caught a big king salmon on our first trip out, but he had been skunked. I had offered Frank a "freebie" the next morning since I was not booked up that day and wanted badly for him to score on a king salmon.

Shortest Trip on Record

Here is what happened on my second trip with Frank Lamberti and it still stands as a personal record today. Frank and I left the dock behind my house at five minutes to six (AM) and motored a short way upriver to the Highway Hole, where we proceeded to back-troll for kings at the guide starting time of 6 AM. Frank had no sooner let his line out when he hooked up a king. We proceeded to drift down the river fighting the big fish and ended up land-ing the king salmon immediately in front of my dock where we tied up and checked the time. It was 6:07 AM and we were done for the day! Frank was thrilled since the fish weighed in at 45 pounds, and he still had the rest of the day to pursue Russian River sockeyes.

Frank faithfully fished with me every one of my 20 years as a Kenai River guide, and has fished with me since as a friend. Frank's annual routine when he has come to the Kenai Peninsula for the past 22 years has been to fish the Kenai River one day (sometimes two), halibut-fish at Homer or Deep Creek, sockeye-fish at Russian River, and dig razor clams at Clam Gulch. Most years Frank came by himself, but once in a while with Lea or a friend or relative. The routine doesn't change much, except over the past ten years or so he has also mixed in a week of gold panning in Western Alaska or Brooks Range. Frank is a good friend, sportsman, and a great character!

Through the Years

Time goes by fast when you're having fun, catching fish, and sharing experiences with friends and clients who come from all over the world. I guess I could write an entire book on "Twenty Years of Guiding on the Kenai," but I won't. Just a few more stories of some memorable times will have to do for this book.

Besides entertaining genuinely good folks day in and day out on my boat, the memorable times are when these same folks have a great experience on the river. There are those clients who are going to have a great time no matter what happens; and then there are those who are destined to have a miserable time short of catching a world-record salmon on a beautiful sunny day. Thankfully, most of my clients fell into the first category.

In all my advertising, and discussions with clients interested in booking a trip, I was careful to never guarantee or oversell a trip. I produced just one basic brochure for the 20 years we were in the business and in it pretty much spelled out the way things were on the Kenai River. I noticed over the years that a lot of guides decided to use my original format, since it was simple and to the point without over hyping the Kenai experience. My approach, and the way I treated clients once they were in my boat, resulted in having to do very little advertising after my first couple of years. Repeats and referrals were the hallmarks of my business for a 20 year period.

Some other guides took a different approach with fancy color brochures, expensive full-page magazine or newspaper ads, and exaggerated claims. Guides wanting to grow "too big for their britches" become not only in need of more and more new clients, but also find themselves annually in need of new, and most often inexperienced, fishing guides to assist with their operations. These guide services must expend large amounts on advertising and on annually working several sportsman's shows in an attempt to fill their boats. It becomes a vicious cycle and often results in an inferior service to their clients because of the burdensome size of their operation and the inexperience of personnel due to a high turnover rate. These are the very types of operations that resist the need, recognized by just about everyone else involved in fishing or managing the Kenai River, to limit the number of guides because of crowding. These are also the very type of operations that are most responsible for giving the Kenai River guide industry a bad reputation.

A Foursome's Birdie

Now I will get off my high horse and get back to a few of the more memorable experiences that I promised to relate. I mentioned the seven minute trip as my personal record for shortest trip to catch one king salmon. This next story is about a personal record to limit out a party of four fishermen on the Kenai. It was on a Tuesday morning in mid-July 1996. Tuesdays in July on the Kenai River are known as *Hot Tuesdays,* because guides are not allowed to fish on Sundays and neither guides nor private powerboat anglers are allowed to fish on Mondays. Thus, there is essentially a two-day buildup of fish in all of the major fishing holes on the lower Kenai and come Tuesday *all hell breaks loose,* at least for the first couple of hours in the morning. This is not always the case, but often so at or near the peak of the run, providing water conditions in the river are good.

On this particular Tuesday morning, my clients were George Cutting and three friends from Homer. George is another good friend, and one of the world's great characters. Being a fellow golfer, George got into an annual routine of fishing with me in the morning and playing a round of golf together in the afternoon. We had left my dock about 5:45 AM and by the 6 AM starting time had baited up and were in position to fish the Sunken Island hole.

My fishing log for that day (I kept a log of every trip for 20 years) indicates there were 25 other boats in the hole that morning and that we hooked up with a double at 6:05 AM. We fought our way through the other boats and managed to land one of the two fish we had hooked, a 40 pound king salmon. Several other boats were fighting fish out of the hole so it looked like we might be in for a good morning. We were soon back in position and hooked and landed another king in the 40 pound class. Two down—two to go. Before 7 AM we had landed our third king and shortly after our fourth, both fish between 35 and 40 pounds. We had now limited out and by 7:30 AM were back to my dock. Actual fishing time was one hour and fifteen minutes and all fish had been caught on small red/chrome spin and glo's with heavily scented salmon eggs. This was the quickest I had ever limited out a party of four and the last time I ever fished the Kenai during a time when bait was allowed that I didn't have a bottle of anise oil or other scent aboard.

Now for the rest of the story. At the time I was working closely with my good friend, golfing partner, and fellow fishing guide Bill Altland. While on the river our routine was to check with each other by cell phone about every hour or so. I had been too busy to answer his call around 7 AM and when I did try to call back his line was busy. It was 9 AM by the time Bill called back and by this time George and I were out on the Birch Ridge golf course. Bill inquired as to where I was and how things were going. When I answered "Bill, I'm at the second hole at Birch Ridge and I birdied the first," there was silence at the other end of the line. When he came back he asked, "What in the world are you talking about, I thought you were fishing today." I explained what had happened that morning, and after that Bill never knew what to believe when I answered his calls!

The Kid Knows the Regs

The biggest fish we ever caught on my boat had to be returned to the water since it was not legally hooked. Kenai River regulations require that any fish not hooked in the mouth had to be released immediately and this fish was snagged in the back. We had been drifting at the Bluffs that day in July, 1992, with a young lad of only seven,—Chris Palm—and his mother, Debbie. Hooking this fish in the deep water slot at the Bluffs, I had no way of knowing that it was snagged and when it stayed down and Chris couldn't budge it, I knew it was big. The big king eventually made some long runs back and forth across the river and after about 30 minutes of this exciting fight by this skilled young boy, I realized it was snagged.

I had neglected to discuss the snagging regulation with Chris and his mom ahead of time and I was feeling really bad about having to break the news to them that they could not retain this fish of a lifetime. Before I told them both the bad news I heard Chris yell out, "Mom, we're going to be letting this one go. It's snagged in the back." Turns out that Chris, even at this young age, was an avid fisherman who knew the sport fishing regulations inside out and there was little surprise or disappointment in having to release this fish.

We brought Chris' fish alongside the boat and quickly took length and girth measurements and a picture—all the time Chris helping me to make sure that the fish stayed in the water. There is a formula that Fish and Game uses to convert length and girth measurements into weight and using this formula Chris' big king would have weighed between 80 and 85 pounds! Chris helped me release the fish and with a big smile on his face asked, "Do we have time to do another drift?"

A New World Record—Not

Every once in a while a rumor gets started on the Kenai River that someone has caught, or is in the process of catching "a new world record king salmon." National media even covered the story of the guy who "fought" a king salmon for 36 hours on the Kenai, only to lose it in the process of netting. While the battle raged on the word got out somehow that this king salmon being fought was going to be a new world record. For sure! Turns out that the actual fight was probably only an hour or so and the rest of the time the guide (new to the river) and his client just hovered over a hole while the fish rested below.

Family Fun

(above left) Uncle Bion Hall proudly displays more than 110 pounds salmon. His first 57 pound king is mounted and hangs on the wall of his son Brad's home.

(above right) Brother Dave and I display a pair of king salmon taken in the lower river on July 31, 1988. Dave caught the bigger one which weighed in at 57 pounds. Mine was "just an average" 45 pound Kenai king.

Sandra's cousin, Eric Ohlson, and his wife Sheri had their lucky day near the Kenai Bridge in early July, 2006. Both fish were sent off to the taxidermist. Photo by Wendy Dutcher

(left) Nearly 40 years after he first took me fishing it was "pay back time" for Uncle Charlie Benson, the "Fish Tutor." His first king salmon.

(lower right) Sandra's Dad, George Kelley, and I net his 42 pound king salmon taken above the Soldotna Bridge in the Highway Hole, July 1988.

(left) Jake Windham and Kenney Kelley (Sandra's brother) hold up Jake's 66 pound king salmon taken at the Cow Pasture, July 1994.

(left)L. to R: Elaine Flagg, Mitch Flagg, and Jean Flavin. Jean (Elaine's sister) was visiting from New York and caught this 40 pound king just above the Warren Ames Bridge in July, 2006.

((below) My Mom, Lucile Benson Flagg, was introduced to Kenai River fishing by her grandson, Mitch. "Lady Luck" held true and Mom landed this 45 pound king salmon at Eagle Rock.

((below) Sandra and I with her early May king salmon, taken from our drift boat just above Porters in 1987. Photo taken by good friend and guide Brad Carver.

Crowds gathered on the bank to watch and coffee and food runs were made out to the boat during the night. Finally they decided to put a little pressure on the fish and the battle was soon brought to conclusion. The final moments were captured on video as the big king, possibly in the 70-to-80 pound class, escaped between the two nets and three guides that were used for the landing this fish. Just another big Kenai king and another big fish story to boot!

An Embarrassing Trophy

Probably the funniest "new world record" story that I was witness to occurred in the mid-'90s on the lower river, and this one involved another Kenai River guide. This guide, who we'll call Ron, was drift fishing with clients near Honeymoon Cove when one of the members of his party hooked into "something big." The water was pretty high and fast at the time making it a little difficult for Ron to judge what was going on as they drifted along fighting the "big fish." The battle continued as they drifted further on down the river on through major fishing holes at the Pillars, the Toilet Hole, and Eagle Rock. By the time they fought their way past the Crossover, and on into the Beaver Creek hole, word was all over the river thanks to cell phones and CB radios: "Ron is fighting a new world-record king salmon!"

I was fishing Beaver Creek at the time and as Ron drifted through the hole, with his client's fishing pole bent over double, he yelled out, "It's huge, we can't move it!" They continued the fight down through the lower river holes past Mud Island, the Bluffs, and on into the Cow Pasture. By this time a couple hours had gone by and Ron and his fisherman were pretty exhausted. A small armada of boats were by now following closely behind to witness the landing of the new "world-record" king salmon.

Soon a shallow sandbar was in sight, but as they drifted toward it the fisherman was still unable to move the fish, try as he might. A potential disaster loomed since they could easily lose this giant in the shallow hazards of the sandbar. As they fought their way into the shoals their quarry became visible for the first time. To everyone's surprise and chagrin, a somewhat rounded and waterlogged tree stump rolled onto the sandbar, a brightly colored red and yellow spin-and-glow lure firmly attached!

The stump had been rolling along the river bottom in the strong river current with hook firmly attached, stopping or slowing now and then in deep water or a hole, suddenly to pick up speed again as it exited a hole back into the stronger current. Behaving just about like a big king might. After landing his "trophy stump" in front of a crowd of observers, Ron was not seen on the river again for several days!

The Rabbi's Blessing

I received a phone call from Rabbi Bruce in the early spring of 2000. The rabbi hailed from the San Francisco area and told me that he had caught many king salmon, but never anything more than about 30 pounds. He made it very clear that his goal in life (at least his fishing life) was to catch a king salmon more than 40 pounds. This was for some reason very important to him and he wanted to know what his chances were on the Kenai River and what was the best time to come. I gave him my honest assessment—that a 40 pound king was not at all an unreasonable goal on the Kenai River. However, there was no guarantee—especially since he had only one day to fish. Also, since I was already well into my booking season, the best date I could offer was July 27, about a week later than the normal peak of the run.

The rabbi didn't book right away and probably called a few other guides to see what they could offer. A week or so later I got another call from Rabbi Bruce with several questions for which he sought out detailed answers. This was not uncommon for prospective new clients and I always thought that one of my strengths was my background as a fisheries biologist who had actually spent several years working on the Kenai River. In addition, by this time I had guided on the Kenai for more than ten years, and had become pretty adept at answering just about any question. But the rabbi had many questions and he called me several more times during the next week before he finally booked the trip. He had a unique way of talking—a very slow cadence and careful pronunciation of each word—similar to the rabbi that appeared on a couple of episodes of the *Seinfeld* TV show. I started to like the rabbi and began to realize just how important it was for him to catch his 40 pound king salmon.

With Rabbi Bruce and three other single clients, including my good friend Frank Lamberti, we headed out on the Kenai River early in the morning on July 27. The rabbi had been in good spirits but as the day wore on he started to look a little depressed. When by noon, and six hours of fishing later, we hadn't even had a bite—the rabbi started to look a mite more glum. We were back-trolling down low in the Cow Pasture and I knew that the tide had turned at the river mouth and was on the way back in. Having recently seen *Fiddler on the Roof,* I recalled the scene where the village rabbi was asked by the persecuted Jews to say a blessing in hopes of improving their desperate situation. So I asked Rabbi Bruce if he would be willing to say a blessing for all of us in the boat in the hopes it might change our luck fishing.

The rabbi obliged and began a Yiddish chant that went on for about a minute. Before I could ask him to interpret the blessing his rod went down and he

Fishing Friends

(left) Our trusty fishing guide Brad Carver with his wife Jeanna (L.) and Brad's Mom Carol (R.) with a pair of bright Kenai River king salmon.

(right) Fisher Lady extraordinair Gert Seekins from Homer and her 65 pound early-run king salmon taken in 1988 at Eagle Rock.

(below) Audrey and Jim Rearden with 70 pounds of early June king salmon caught in the College and Highway Hole's. 1988. Jim was my first supervisor at Fish & Game in the late 1960s.

The Chihuly gals from Ninilchik with a nice limit of Kenai silvers. L. to R: Michelle, Shirley (Mom), Irene Nelson, and Theresa.

The Walker/Hughes gang with a quick limit of kings from Sunken Island. L. to R: Laurie Hughes (62 pounds), Buddy Hughes (45 pounds), Judy Walker (50 pounds), and Rob Walker (40 pounds)

Debbie Burwin and Sandra with a pair of nice kings from the lower river. "Sonar Debbie" works for ADF&G and is the project leader for the Kenai River king salmon sonar counter.

(left) George Cutting and friends from Homer (and Oyster Bay, N.Y.) with their "90 minute limit" of kings taken at Sunken Island, July 1996.

(below) My best friend from high school and college years, Ned Handy, pays a visit from the Bay State and catches his first king salmon.

(above) Late season mixed bag—3 kings and a silver. L. to R: Bob Och, Loren, and Dave Waite. Bob and Dave both worked with me at ADF&G.

(below) Setting out with a party of friends for another fishing trip on the "world famous" Kenai River.

was obviously hooked into a big fish. About 15 minutes later the rabbi was all smiles, back in his seat after landing a 43 pound king salmon, the fish of his dreams. He was about to relate to us the meaning of his blessing when Chuck's rod went down, this time a 53 pound king. After landing this fish we set up to back troll-again and immediately Gene hooked up and proceeded to land a 30 pound king. This was all happening too fast and the Rabbi still hadn't told his story. Only Frank was left and it's quite often difficult to get that last fish, since you only have one line in the water competing against the several hundred lines from the other boats around you. But not this time! Frank hooked up and landed a 25 pound king and knowing from experience how hard it can be to get the last fish, and being a good sport, elected to keep it.

We had now limited out in a 90 minute span immediately following the rabbi's blessing and had yet to hear the meaning. "Just what was the meaning of your blessing?" I finally asked. "Well," the Rabbi said, " I was simply asking the Lord to bless the fish and to bless the fishermen and to find a way for the two to be joined together." I imagine that Rabbi Bruce has used this little fish story many times over the years in his talks to his followers.

Ladies, Kids, and Old Geezers

One of the really fun parts about guiding is getting to see a gal catch her first king salmon, a kid catch his first fish ever, or an older man who has fished all his life catch his biggest fish ever. These are the trips you tend to remember and hopefully capture on film for all time.

With the ladies I have observed a very interesting phenomenon over the years—they *almost always* out- fish the men. A guy, a real "sport" who has fished all over the world, will bring his wife along to fish with him on the Kenai. She might care less about the fishing and is along for the company and to enjoy the scenery. He wants in the worst way to catch one of the big kings that the Kenai River is renowned for. I have seen this happen so many times it is quite predictable—the lady will invariably catch the largest king and if there is only one fish to be caught that day, you can bet the ranch on the fact that she will be the one to catch it! You could call it "Lady Luck," but it might also have to do with the fact that ladies tend to listen to instructions from their guides, while some men have a preconceived idea of what to do based on fishing elsewhere, and tend to block out any helpful hints when the moment of truth arrives.

With young kids it's always a thrill—for them, for their parents, and for the guide. The kids can be seen wearing the biggest smiles of their lives and the parents a look of pride. It has been especially enjoyable for me to see my two grandsons, Lee and Eric Kempf, catch their first big fish on the Kenai River. Lee's was a 14 pound silver and Eric's a beautiful 12 pound rainbow.

Another special moment occurs when an elderly gentleman, who has spent a lifetime fishing, comes to the Kenai and catches his biggest fish ever. Sometimes it is even the biggest fish he has ever seen. To see *an old geezer* light up upon catching a big king is a very special thrill. My Uncle Bion Hall and I experienced one of these moments together. Bion was nearly 80 at the time, had fished all his life, but had never hooked into anything near the likes of a big Kenai king salmon.

I took Uncle Bion down into a drift just below Sunken Island, where he hooked and landed a 57 pound king salmon. The next day we drifted this same hole and damned if Bion didn't catch another big king of exactly the same size—57 pounds! This hole, located just above Poacher's Cove, is now named "Uncle Bion's Hole," and displayed proudly on the wall of his son Brad's home in West Yarmouth, Massachusetts is a beautifully mounted silver bright 57 pound Kenai River king salmon.

Chapter 14
Commercial Fishing Conflicts

I was involved in managing the Upper Cook Inlet gill net salmon fishery for a seven-year period starting in 1968. The last couple of years I was the area man-

The Excalibur and two other gill netters return to the Kenai River mouth following a fishing period. The shore "dippers" are out in force.

agement biologist and thus the person responsible for decisions regarding this fishery. There were serious conflicts before I came on board, during my tenure, and after I left the Commercial Fisheries Division in 1974. With more than half the state's population residing in and around the Cook Inlet area and several interests competing for the salmon resource, there will always be conflicts. None of these conflicts is probably more long running and more intense than that of the battle between East Side Cook Inlet set net fishermen and sport fishermen (including guides) over Kenai River bound king salmon.

In February 1968 I was introduced to the nature of this conflict by the first person I met upon arrival in Alaska—none other than Bob Penney, a wealthy businessman and longtime sportfishing advocate. My first day in Anchorage I had gone to Penney Trailer Sales to check into a possible purchase of a house trailer, thinking that I might not find otherwise suitable housing in Homer. Mr. Penney was cordial and we talked trailers for about one minute until he discovered that I was about to go to work for the Commercial Fisheries Division of ADF&G in Homer. Boy, did I get an earful after that! I recall that he said something to the effect that killing a Kenai River king salmon in a commercial set net was akin to cutting down a redwood tree. Mr. Penney and I would find ourselves on opposite sides in this battle between commercial and sportfishermen for the next 30 years.

Set Netting through College

My son, Mitch, landed a job on Nick Leman's set net site in Ninilchik when he was 14 years old. Daughter Laurie was added to the crew after graduation from high school. They both worked summers on the site during their college years

There is work to be done between commercial fishing periods. Laurie is shown here doing one her favorite chores—mending nets!

and for a few years after. This was a great summer job—being outside, earning decent money, and working for one of the finest families we have ever known in Alaska. Nick Leman was born in Ninilchik and had been a commercial fisherman since the late 1920s. His wife, Marian, and sons Wayne, Loren, and Mark all helped run the family's set net sites a couple of miles north of the Ninilchik River.

Mitch got back into the set net fishery later on in 1998 when he and a family friend, Tom Maughan, purchased sites at Clam Gulch from Dick and Molly Musgrove. It turned out to be a great experience for family and friends who participated in running the operation. Tom's son Doug, also a partner, returned to Alaska each summer to help out at the peak of the run, along with one of Mitch's friends, Tim Tingstad. Sandra and I made several trips down to the site each season to help out where we could and to take part in the ever present beach cookouts. There was a small A-frame cabin built right on the beach that supported the fishing operation. Our first trip down to the site was usually in the early spring when we checked out the condition of the cabin and also dug a few razor clams. As far as the salmon fishing went, the guys got off to a good start the first year, but because of a combination of poor prices and a decrease in the number of sockeye hitting this stretch of beach, the site did not turn a profit and was sold back after five years.

The Flagg/Maughan set net site at Clam Gulch along the east side of Cook Inlet. 2000.

King Salmon Conflict

I came to appreciate the hard work and lifestyle that the many families up and down the east side beaches of Cook Inlet had enjoyed and become accustomed to for many years. Families like the Lemans, Musgroves, and others up and down the beach were long-time Alaskans who contributed to the economy year around. To me, these hard working folks were the "salt of the earth." So I guess I became a little sensitive when a new group of fishermen came along—many newly arrived from the lower 48—and attempted to put these longtime Alaskan folks out of business. This new group of Kenai River guides (many nonresidents or new arrivals) had been joining forces with Bob Penney's group, the Kenai River Sportfishing Association (KRSA), to put additional pressure on the setnetters. The basis of the conflict was that set net fishermen along the east side of Cook Inlet were intercepting too many Kenai River bound king salmon while trying to catch their target fish, sockeye. Some of the measures that these sport fishing groups had proposed to the Alaska Board of Fish (BOF) would have effectively put these set net fishermen out of business. In fact, that was the goal of certain leaders of these groups.

Back to the Battle

Within a year of retiring from ADF&G I began to realize that I needed something else to do besides guide on the Kenai River. So when Cheryl Sut-

Tim Tingstad holds boat and a net load of salmon along the beach while waiting for crew to arrive with beach truck.

ton from the Kenai Peninsula Fishermen's Association (KPFA) approached me to assist with their group, I was ready to go back to work. In the fall of 1988 I became executive director for KPFA, which is an organization of Cook Inlet commercial fishermen, mostly setnetters from the east side beaches. From my work with Fish and Game I knew their issues well and was familiar with the data they needed to support their cause, which at this point in time was sim-

110

ply to exist. They were getting close to being put out of business forever.

For the next eight years I worked for KPFA, representing their interests at BOF meetings and other organizations, such as the Kenai River Special Management Area board and the Cook Inlet Aquaculture board. One of my first projects in 1989 was to work with the local fish and game biologists to develop a biologically based king salmon escapement goal for the Kenai River. An excessively high goal had been proposed to the BOF which would have resulted in severe and unnecessary restrictions to both the sport and commercial fisheries. We presented a more rational and biologically based goal to the BOF, which they adopted at the 1989 meeting. This goal has stood the test of time and is essentially the same used today.

I also helped KPFA develop stipulations for proposed oil and gas exploration and development in Cook Inlet, which in some cases threatened to

Another beautiful day on Cook Inlet. Laurie, Mitch, and Chris picking sockeye off the back deck of the Excalibur.

encroach upon their immediate fishing areas. On these and other types of proposed development issues such as logging, we worked closely with Theo Matthews and the United Cook Inlet Drift Association (UCIDA).

Drift Conflicts

Drift gill net fishermen, represented by UCIDA, have been involved in an entirely different conflict, although still involving salmon interception. The 500+ drift gill net boat fleet fishes mainly out in the middle of Cook Inlet, instead of along the beach like the setnetters. My son-in-law, Chris Kempf owns the *Excalibur* and is a "highliner" in this fishery, which is also embroiled in an ongoing conflict with sport and personal use fishermen. "Drifters" are accused of intercepting too many "northern bound" salmon, mostly silvers and sockeyes, in their efforts to adequately harvest the total inlet sockeye return. They are very closely regulated and often kept from fishing in the mid-inlet and are confined to a narrow corridor along the east side where they target just Kenai and/or Kasilof bound fish.

Kodiak Intercept

One issue that KPFA and UCIDA worked closely on was the intercept of Cook Inlet- bound sockeye salmon in the Kodiak area. In the mid to late '80s Kodiak seine fishermen had changed their historic pattern of fishing inner bays

The Excalibur, one of the nicest boats in the Cook Inlet drift gill-net fleet, is owned by one of the best skippers—highliner Chris Kempf.

for pink salmon to targeting Cook Inlet- bound sockeye off their capes. A major battle occurred over the next several years between Kodiak seiners and Cook Inlet gill-netters. Inlet fishermen won round one of this battle in 1990 when the Board of Fish closed the northern portion of Shelikof Straits (the major intercept area), but lost round two in 1995 when an attempt was made to get some of the other intercept areas to the south of the straits closed down.

This was a classic fish war which raged on for several years and four major BOF meetings, all having standing room only for participants. As executive director for KPFA, I found myself smack in the middle of this highly contentious and stressful fish fight. In the end, the issue was decided by politics, rather than biological and fishery management concerns. The decision by the BOF to allow the Kodiak seine fishery to target and harvest Cook Inlet bound sockeye salmon south of Shelikof Straits went against Alaska's own mixed stock management policy

King Salmon Fund

One of the projects I implemented for KPFA was the King Salmon Fund. Setnetters were losing the public relations battle over the intercept of Kenai River king salmon at the very time Kenai River habitat issues were coming to the forefront. I saw an opportunity to not only assist in the PR battle, but to do some good for the habitat issue at the same time. The plan was for set net fishermen to donate the proceeds from the king salmon they incidentally caught in their nets, while targeting sockeye, to a fund dedicated to habitat

Tom and Doug Maughan await slack tide to finish "picking" their set nets at the Clam Gulch site.

protection. Since fishermen who signed up for this voluntary program would not benefit monetarily, they might also be encouraged to release any live king salmon caught in their nets back to the water.

The plan was implemented in 1992 and worked well for the first couple of years. The fund was set up and a board of directors, independent from KPFA, was established to administer the fund. Several thousand dollars was raised and the money utilized to raise awareness of habitat issues on the river. The King Salmon Fund contributed to the early start of the Kenai River Salmon Festival (which has become an annual event) and also published a beautiful full-color brochure of the Kenai River system and its tributaries. This effort by commercial fishermen was also instrumental in inspiring other organizations, including KRSFA, to implement habitat protection programs in the

Kenai River drainage. Unfortunately, after the third year most fishermen had dropped out of the program because of poor economic conditions at the time and the perception that their efforts were not helping much on the PR front or in decisions made by the BOF.

An Interrupted Season

Very little commercial fishing was done in Cook Inlet in 1989 because of the *Exxon Valdez* oil spill in Prince William Sound. KPFA sent me to the scene of the crime on March 28, 1989.

Chapter 15
Fool's Folly: Exxon Valdez Oil Spill

I was working for the Kenai Peninsula Fishermen's Association (KPFA) in Soldotna when the *Exxon Valdez* grounded on Bligh Reef in Prince William Sound on March 24, 1989, spilling more than 11 million gallons of oil. The spill stayed pretty much in the vicinity of the vessel for the first two days but on the third day strong southeasterly winds began to move the oil into the western part of the Sound, thus creating a potential hazard for the outer coast of the Kenai Peninsula. On March 28, as the oil began to flow in a southerly direction through the Sound, KPFA decided to send me to Valdez to assess the potential threat from the oil spill to the Cook Inlet area.

Eric Barnes, one of our KPFA members, flew me to the Sound just after noon on the 28th of March in his Cessna 180. We flew through Port Nellie Juan and observed no oil there but as we approached Knight Island we saw clearly the leading edge of the oil slick immediately north of Herring Bay. As we flew along the edge of this tremendous mass of oil, tears unexpectedly welled up in my eyes as I saw dozens of seals and sea otters and hundreds of marine birds in the immediate path. I knew these critters were toast and at that time the true reality of this disaster hit me squarely. I had a strong feeling then that Prince William Sound, and the lives of those who depended on its tremendously productive waters, would never be the same again.

We continued on through the northern part of the Sound and then flew over the *Exxon Valdez* at 2:15 PM. I wrote in my field notebook that oil was still escaping from the boom surrounding the tanker, four days after the initial spill. Eric dropped me off in Valdez and that evening I attended the briefing by state, federal, and Exxon officials. At this meeting I was to hear the first of many Exxon lies to come when a company official stated that everything was under control and that no more oil was escaping from the area around the vessel. Eric and I knew better and had the pictures to prove it.

For the next two days I stayed in Valdez and consulted with state and federal officials on measures being taken to contain and clean up the spill and to assess the potential threat to Cook Inlet and Kachemak Bay. Spill trackers from the Department of Environmental Conservation (DEC) predicted that the oil would exit through Montague Sound and then follow a course along the outer coast of the Kenai Peninsula and eventually threaten Cook Inlet. NOAA officials were predicting that the oil would go offshore into the Gulf

Exxon Valdez oil spill, Prince William Sound, Alaska. March, 1989. Photo courtesy of USGS.

of Alaska and that the threat to the Kenai Peninsula was minimal. Recalling circulation models developed by the University of Alaska and reports on nutrient transport from Prince William Sound to Cook Inlet, I chose to believe the DEC prediction and immediately alerted the Kenai Peninsula Borough in Soldotna, the Alaska Department of Fish and Game in Homer, and the Institute of Marine Science in Seward.

By early April it became clear that the DEC oil spill trajectory model was correct and that the Cook Inlet area was about to become a victim of the oil spill. On April 7, Kenai Peninsula Borough Mayor Don Gilman formed a Multi-Agency Coordination Advisory Council in Homer and appointed me as chairman. The Homer MAC team (HMAC) was made up of federal, state, borough, city, village, and citizen representatives. We established as our first objective the protection of fishery resources in the outer and southern districts of the Cook Inlet Management Area west of Nuka Island. We also identified needs for the Homer area, which included oil containment and cleanup equipment, experts in oil spill cleanup, marine mammal and bird surveys, experts in marine mammal and bird cleaning, and a vessel cleaning station in the Kachemak Bay area.

Where was Exxon?

One of the real disappointments in the early stages of our response effort out of Homer was the inability of Exxon to provide an expert in oil spill cleanup to the area. After repeated requests from HMAC, an Exxon representative finally showed up in Homer on April 10. However, to everyone's dismay it turned out to be a retired public relations company man who had never been to Alaska and had no experience in oil spill cleanup! To me this was simply unforgivable and showed Exxon's callousness and lack of understanding of the situation. Furthermore, it led to a lack of progress in obtaining badly needed boom and other oil spill equipment to fight the mass of oil that was now entering several bays in the Outer District of the Cook Inlet Management Area. These bays supported several major salmon streams that were the backbone of the seine fishery for fishermen living in Homer and Seldovia as well as the Native villages of Port Graham and English Bay.

Citizen Action

The inability of Exxon to obtain oil spill boom or otherwise provide any meaningful help led to citizen action on two fronts. First of all, commercial fishermen and loggers around the Kachemak Bay formed an alliance and started building protective booms in both Homer and Seldovia. Citizens had felt hopeless and needed something to do to fight the spill and keep it from getting into salmon streams and other sensitive areas. An attempt was even made to close off all of Seldovia Bay using a combination of log boom and other materials. Schools were closed to allow kids to assist by filling sandbags. As the spill progressed into Kachemak Bay and folks began to realize that the defenses were inadequate, frustration, and in some cases panic set in. One Seldovia city official was said to be running around the village much like Jonathon Winters in the 1966 movie, *The Russians Are Coming, the Russians Are Coming.*

An Attempted Coup

Frustration led to anger and anger led to more citizen action, this time on the political front. A group of commercial fishermen and other Kachemak Bay citizens confronted Congressman Don Young and Senator Ted Stevens when they came to Homer on April 21 to assess the progress of the oil spill response effort. At 9:30 AM that day I was called out of our Homer MAC meeting at the request of Congressman Young and ushered into the middle of this highly contentious meeting between Young, Exxon, the U.S. Coast Guard, and the band of protesting citizens. As I sat down at the table, the first thing Congressmen Young said to me was "Mr. Flagg, we want you to be in charge of the oil spill!" I asked for someone to please tell me what the hell was going on, and found out the citizens were attempting a coup against Exxon and wanted them out of the way. Since the Coast Guard had already decided that the spill would not be federalized, Young, prompted by the citizen committee, was looking for an alternative to run the show and I had been nominated.

I suggested to Congressman Young and the others, that if Exxon would provide adequate funding to the Kenai Peninsula Borough, more progress could be made in obtaining needed supplies and initiating action to respond to the spill. Later, at lunch, Young and I were joined by KPB Mayor Gilman and Secretary of the Interior Lujan to discuss a course of action. We developed a proposed plan at this meeting and then met over dinner with Senator Stevens to brief him on the situation and obtain his approval. Mayor Gilman then met with Exxon officials, and with pressure applied from Young and Stevens, was able to get a commitment from Exxon for $2.0 million for the KPB to fight the spill.

The next day was spent finalizing response plans and actions that the KPB would take utilizing the pledged money from Exxon. But by early afternoon that day Exxon had reneged on their offer of $2.0 million and was now offering only $1.0 million and with strings attached! After further negotiations, during which most of the strings were snipped, Mayor Gilman accepted the offer and we were able to get to work.

With the money now in hand, our first priority was to order containment boom and within two days we had received 5000 feet of commercial-grade boom in Homer. At that point we came to the full realization that Exxon had been giving us the runaround since they had been telling us that there was no boom available "anywhere in the world." I don't know if it was deception or total incompetence, but it was amazing to me that one of the world's largest oil companies had been unable to obtain the equipment needed to respond to this spill. They had said it was all in use in Prince William Sound, but this simply wasn't true. They simply hadn't tried hard enough nor attempted to use resources other than their usual vendors. And their main point man in Homer was still the retired PR guy!

Oil Enters Kachemak Bay

The fight to protect Kachemak Bay, the Outer District, and the rest of Cook Inlet continued through the spring, summer, and on into the fall. At times things got a little better as Exxon and the Homer MAC team started to get in more equipment, including much needed containment boom, to fight the spill—which by mid April had entered the outer reaches of Kachemak Bay. Skimmers and barges were needed just about everywhere and when there simply weren't enough to go around frustration would set in again. Priorities were set and most of the major salmon streams eventually received containment boom. However, in some cases, because of delays, the booms arrived way too late to protect these streams and they were trashed. In other cases weather, mainly strong winds, tore up the booms and oil flowed on into the streams or other critical areas that were being protected.

Many commercial fishermen and Natives from the villages were eventually hired by Exxon to help with the spill. Others simply did things on their own, not wanting anything to do with the big oil company that had screwed things up so badly. Bird-and otter-cleaning stations were set up with some help from Exxon, and some volunteer assistance. A group of citizens took over a beach cleaning project at Gore Point and spent the summer and early fall hand scrubbing rocks and digging up the sand in an effort to clean this heavily polluted beach. Billy Day, the leader of this volunteer effort, even built a washing machine for oiled rocks out of his own funds. It worked quite well and the group of volunteers moved on to clean up another beach at Mars Cove during the fall.

Commercial Fishery Closed

A huge impact from the spill came during the summer months when most of Cook Inlet was closed to commercial fishing because of the presence of oil. Tar balls had floated up the inlet and into the areas fished by the Cook Inlet drift fleet and into areas fished by set net fishermen along the beach. The state had a zero-tolerance policy in effect for oil and could not take the chance that even a small portion of the salmon harvest would become contaminated. Thus, most commercial fishermen were shut down for the season and an over-escapement of salmon was allowed into the rivers, eventually resulting in damage to these systems. Although Exxon partially compensated fishermen for the loss of fishing time during the 1989 season, many fishermen felt, justifiably so, that the impacts and resulting losses were far greater than the compensation—and extended far into future seasons.

CIRCAC

Responding to the *Exxon Valdez* disaster, Congress passed an Oil Pollution Act in 1990, providing tougher standards for oil spill readiness and prevention. One of the OPA 90 provisions mandated that citizen advisory councils for oil industry oversight be established in Prince William Sound and Cook Inlet. The Cook Inlet Regional Citizens Advisory Council (CIRCAC) was established in October 1990 and initially formed two working committees— the Environmental Monitoring Committee and the Prevention, Response, Operations, and Safety (PROPS) committee.

I was appointed to the PROPS committee in 1990 and we immediately went to work on several projects. The primary focus of PROPS was on projects and studies that provided a basis for recommendations aimed at minimizing oil spill risks in Cook Inlet. A second objective was to review and monitor oil spill response efforts and developments in best available technology.

Over the next few years, PROPS was involved in several projects including safety of navigation, development of oil spill trajectory models, participation in industry oil spill drills, review of oil spill contingency plans, and development of geographic response strategies. Since I had the background from my years of working on the Kachemak Bay and Lower Cook Inlet marine study, I took the lead on the mapping of critical habitat areas that would be in line for priority protection in the event of an oil spill.

PetroPiscis

Early in 1992, the CIRCAC board of directors appointed me to represent the council at the Second International Conference on Fisheries and Offshore Petroleum Exploration in Bergen, Norway. I had attended the first international conference in the fall of 1989, and had given attendees a brief preliminary report on the *Exxon Valdez* oil spill. This time I was to present a more formal paper, which was titled *Cook Inlet Alaska: A 30 Year History of Commercial Fishing and Oil Industries Operating Concurrently in an Offshore Subarctic Environment.* This 29 page report, presented in April, 1992, described the Cook Inlet area, the history of the two industries, the conflicts that had occurred, the high risks that were present, stipulations designed to minimize impacts, new regulations that had developed post *Exxon Valdez*, and finally, the future outlook for the area.

In the conclusion of the report, I outlined recommendations for further prevention measures for the Cook Inlet oil industry. Several measures were based on recommendations from the Alaska Oil Spill Commission and from the *Safety of Navigation* report that CIRCAC had commissioned. Now, more than 15 years later, some of these safety recommendations for the Cook Inlet oil industry have finally been implemented. Others, however, have not and there is still room for improvement. The words spoken to the Seattle Fish Expo in 1989 by former Alaska Department of Environmental Conservation Commissioner Dennis Kelso are still haunting. Kelso then said: *"Cook Inlet is a disaster waiting to happen."*

Chapter 16
Just for the Halibut

When you live in the Kenai/Soldotna area and want to go halibut fishing there are several options available. Homer, Deep Creek, and Seward all offer excellent guide services and boat launch facilities. Deep Creek and Anchor Point offer a tractor launch option. I used to launch my Bay Runner off the beach at Deep Creek, but since my 20-foot Koffler is a heavier boat I now use the tractor launch service. Up until just a few years ago the cost for this service was $30, but it has now gone up to $50. This is still not too bad if you are sharing the expense with two or three of your fishing buddies.

Halibut fishing is available out of the Deep Creek area for about six months of the year, but most small boat-fishermen limit their efforts to a four-month period from May through August. Wind is a critical factor and we always call down to the tractor launch to get a report on sea conditions before we make the one-hour tow from Kenai down to the beach at Deep Creek. Tides are also important and although the "bite" can be good for a short window of time on the extreme tides, we usually plan our trips around the small neap tides. The smaller tides allow a longer period of time to fish while anchored up without having to use a ridiculous amount of weight to hold the bottom.

A Memorable Trip

The story that follows is an account of one of our more memorable recent trips down to Deep Creek for halibut fishing. On July 7, 2007, the high tide at Deep Creek was a 16 footer at 9AM; however, actual high slack at the hole we fished offshore would not occur until 90 minutes later. Our fishing party that day consisted of my brother David Flagg, his wife, Donna Flagg, my grandson Lee Kempf, and first mate Scott Kempf. Dave and Donna hailed from Pittsburgh, Pennsylvania. We gathered our troops at 7 AM and made the one hour tow down to Deep Creek, where we used the tractor launch service. We brought along our salmon gear, as well as halibut gear, and for the first hour or so trolled along the beach for kings at Twin Falls. It turned out to be a slow day for king salmon so we headed out to "Rich's Hole" and got anchored up while the tide was still running strong. This hole, in about 90 feet of water, was named for my good friend and fishing partner, Rich Hill,

Results from a memorable trip to Cook Inlet for my brother and his wife. L. to R: Scott with his (and Donna's) 150 pound halibut, Donna Flagg, Lee Kempf, David Flagg, and the skipper. July, 2007.

who passed away in 2005 after a year-long battle with colon cancer. Rich and I had been fishing this hole for about three years before he died and had always done well, usually limiting out on decent sized halibut.

After we located the hole using GPS, Scott attached a baited scent bag to the anchor line and dropped the hook. We each baited up with half a herring, attached 20-ounce weights, and let out the line. The tide was still running too strong even though it was well past book time for high slack. We reeled our lines back in and attached 30 ounce weights, which found the bottom about 100 feet behind the boat. Fishing was slow at first but we managed to pull in a couple of small "chicken" halibut. After about 30 minutes the tide began to slow and we changed to lighter weights. Shortly after, Donna yelled out, "I got one," and proceeded to pull in about a 30 pound halibut, our first keeper. She couldn't get over how big it was, possibly her biggest fish ever, but Scott and I kidded her that it was just a baby as far as Alaska halibut were concerned.

The action was fair to middling for the next hour or so while the tide was slack. We released several more chickens and everyone on the boat kept one halibut in the 25 to 30 pound range. Since the limit is two halibut, we usually keep our first good-sized ones and then hold out until later in the trip in an effort to land a bigger fish. Then the tide began to change and, as we have always experienced in the past, the action picked up. No more chicken-sized halibut—the fish were now running a little bigger. We kept a couple in the 40 pound class and then I hooked into something really big. The big fish ran about half my line off the reel, then turned and the hook pulled out. "Oh shoot, I wanted to see that fish!" Donna exclaimed.

The action slowed a little, but we still had three fish to go for our limit. Donna asked me to hold her rod while she dug a sandwich out of the cooler. Scott's rod then went down and he was hooked on to something really big. Seconds later the rod I was holding for Donna went down and this was a big one also. Then it appeared our two lines were going out in the same direction and sure enough, we were hooked onto the same fish. Scott did most of the work, pumping and reeling the fish back in, as he had hooked up first. Donna took her rod back from me and fought the fish for a minute or two, just to experience what a big fish feels like. After about 15 minutes we got our first look and Donna, recalling the line from the movie *Jaws,* cried out, "We're *gonna need a bigger boat!"*

Where's the Gun?

Big halibut are what we call "shooters," since it common practice to dispatch these fish with a gunshot before they are brought into a boat, especially a small boat. The problem is that these big flatfish go wild once out of the water and can make a terrible mess out of your boat, as well as cause serious injury. Broken legs have occurred and there are some instances where halibut have caused fishermen to be knocked out of the boat, resulting in drowning. Now, at this point I must add that it was Scott's assigned job to bring along the gun for this trip. As Scott and Donna brought the big halibut closer to the edge of the boat I asked Scott "Where's the gun?" Much to my surprise and concern Scott answered, "Oh damn, I forgot to bring it!"

And so the fun began. I grabbed the harpoon, which is another important

Just for the Halibut

(upper left) The Kenai River is full of surprise. Just kidding! Rich Hill (center), Scott Kempf (R.) and I display a nice catch of halibut and a small salmon taken at Deep Creek, but cleaned at Poacher's Cove on the Kenai 2004.

(upper right) Scott Kempf, Dave Litchfield, and I with our three biggest halibut from an early morning trip on Cook Inlet. Mine weighed in at 125 pounds.

(above) Not all trips to Deep Creek result in bragging sized halibut. My good buddy and fishing partner Rich Hill shares a special moment with his son, Michael, following another Cook Inlet halibut adventure. 2004.

(right) Garret Williams displays his first Alaska halibut. Author's Koffler boat with new canvas top is in the background.

tool needed for landing big halibut, and tied a line tethering it off to the stern of the boat. The big halibut was brought up alongside the boat and I drove the harpoon into its head just behind the eyes. All hell broke loose! The halibut proceeded to make several high-speed circles out to the length of the line attaching the harpoon to the boat, splashing seawater all over us during the process. After a couple of minutes she (most big halibut are females) settled down a bit and came up alongside the boat where we now saw the two hooks in its mouth. I tried to gaff it, but it tore off on another run, yanking the gaff from my hand and sinking it to the bottom. "Now what?" Scott inquired. "Let's try my fish bonker," I responded. Scott is taller, and, having a better reach over the side of the boat, was chosen for the task. While I held his rod, he proceeded to beat the halibut in the head using the fish bonker and all his strength. When it was finally subdued, we hauled it aboard and laid it on the bottom of the boat. To our surprise, it was not done yet, and began the classic head to tail "halibut flop," scattering gear as well as fishermen. Scott beat it in the head a few more times and we then threw it into the fish box where its tail stuck out a foot or so.

We proceeded to limit out with a couple of 30 pounders and then headed back in, toting more than 400 pounds of halibut. The fish was caught on both Scott, and Donna's lines, but Scott got major bragging rights since he had hooked up first. Not finding an adequate scale, we had to rely on the length/weight relationship found in the back of most tide books. The halibut may not have been that big by Alaska standards, but at 66 inches and 150 pounds was big enough to provide a memorable trip and, along with the other halibut caught, a good year's supply of halibut steaks for all aboard that day. Just another day of fishing *just for the halibut* in Cook Inlet, Alaska!

Chapter 17
Kenai Sportfishing Medley

In earlier chapters I have tried to give some insight into sportfishing opportunities and adventures available around Kachemak Bay, Cook Inlet, and the Kenai River. The chapter on the Kenai River dealt mainly with guided trips for king salmon. This next chapter relates a few other memorable sport fishing experiences along the Kenai River system that I have been fortunate to take part in during my years in Alaska.

Russian River Sockeyes

I first fished the Russian for sockeyes in 1968. Even back then it was terribly crowded, but at least you could sometimes find a rock to stand on. There are some people who don't seem to mind

A limit of sockeye salmon on the Russian River. L. to R: Frank Lamberti, Lea Lamberti, Sandra Flagg, and guide Loren. June, 1989.

the crowded conditions in the lower Russian, and in fact, actually enjoy the circus atmosphere. I've found that these folks all tend to be from New York City! Just kidding, but I would bet that a social study of participants who enjoy this fishery would reveal a strong bias toward certain personality types.

At the peak of the sockeye salmon run the lower Russian River, near the confluence with the Kenai River, is to me a place to avoid at all costs. Since I still enjoy catching sockeye in the Russian, I've found it necessary to keep close tabs on the progress of the run and when fish finally make their inevitable move to the upper reaches of the river, it's time to grab the fishing gear and go. It's all about the timing and can be hit or miss, but if you can catch it just right the fishing can be phenomenal.

One of our more memorable trips to the upper Russian was in 1989 with our good friends, Frank and Lea Lamberti. The early sockeye return was so strong that year that Fish and Game opened the area above the falls to sportfishing. This area is seldom opened, but when it is, fantastic fishing can be had. Sandra and I and the Lamberti's hiked up on the Russian Lake trail to a point between the falls and the fish weir. Since the area had just been opened and the word hadn't gotten out to everyone, we shared the fishing hole with just two other parties.

The sockeye fishing was as good as it gets and in this clear, fast water the fish were aggressively pursuing and taking our flies. This was definitely not a "snag in the corner of the mouth" operation, as is most of the sockeye harvest in the Kenai system. Once in a while in certain situations, sockeye will actively bite, and this was one of those times. Frank and I hooked and released until our arms were sore while the girls were content to catch their 3-fish limit and call it a day. By the time we had all limited out and other fishing parties had found their way to the hole, it was time to quit or risk ruining the experience, which was about to become another fishing circus. As I said, it's all a matter of timing, and with Russian River sockeye fishing, timing is critical.

Kenai River Silvers

Fishing for silver salmon, or cohos, in the Kenai River is a lot more laid back than the zoo the Kenai River king salmon fishery has become. With silvers, which run from late July through October, the modus operandi is to find a good spot along the bank of the river and "drop the hook," or in land lubber terms, lower the anchor. Once anchored, you bait your hook with salmon eggs and then, adding the appropriate amount of weight—usually 2-or 3-ounces—either let out the line or cast off behind the boat. You then simply sit back, relax, and wait for a school of silvers to work their way up the river and hopefully find your bait. There are other ways to do it, such as back-trolling with plugs or casting hardware (metal lures), but bait fishing is by far the most popular method.

As with king salmon, or any other kind of fishing, the most fun occurs when you bring kids along. My grandson Lee was just 4-years-old when we brought him along on his first salmon fishing trip on the lower Kenai. We anchored up one beautiful September day along the grassy bank just above the Bluffs and let our lines out behind the boat. We had hoped to hook Lee up with just an average sized 6-to-8 pound silver for his first fish ever, but when his rod went down and line started screaming off the reel, I knew we were onto something bigger. His mom and dad, Laurie and Chris, were aboard and shouted out encouragement as Lee struggled trying to work the reel.

My grandson, Lee Kempf, with his first silver salmon—a 14 pound beauty and our biggest silver of the year. 1998.

The rod itself remained securely set in the rod holder since Lee was still a little too young and inexperienced to handle a fish of this size. We just let him crank away on the reel and offered little help since he was determined to bring his first-ever fish in all by himself. After about ten minutes Lee brought the beautiful bright silver alongside the boat where I was able to net it for him.

We all caught some other nice silvers that day but Lee's was special as not only his very first fish but also the biggest of the day and the biggest we caught that year, weighing in at 14 pounds! We took some pictures at the dock and

131

when the Soldotna Chamber of Commerce later asked me for a photo to use in their new brochure, we submitted one that Sandra had taken of Lee and Gramps with Lee's big silver at the dock. The Chamber folks liked it so much that they used it for the next several years in their annual leaflets, brochures, and other advertising outlets.

Kenai Rainbows

Just off the dock behind our house on the Kenai River was a great rainbow trout hole. Over the 25 years that we lived on the river, our family and friends enjoyed the easy access and consistently good fishing that this hole offered. Rainbows in the 5-to-10 pound class were not uncommon at all and occasionally even larger rainbows were taken. The record for the largest rainbow landed near our dock goes to one of our neighbors, Gary Barnes. Gary is also the editor of *Alaska Outdoor Journal* and an avid sport fisherman. In July 1990 Gary was fishing out back when he hooked and landed a 17.25-pound rainbow, the state record for that year. The fish measured just more than 30 inches. The following week I was fishing for sockeye off the dock when I hooked into my biggest rainbow ever—a 29 inch beauty—which I released.

Gary Barnes, our neighbor on the Kenai, displays his 17 1/4 pound rainbow. Gary is owner and editor of Alaska Outdoor Journal website.

We released nearly all the rainbows we caught out back and encouraged others who fished off our dock to do so. The only exceptions were either when a youngster caught a nice one that mom or dad needed to see, or if the angler wanted to have a skin mount made of a trophy-sized fish. My grandson, Eric Kempf, was just 6-years-old when he came down to the dock with his brother and a friend one July afternoon in 2004. I rigged him up a light spinning rod and helped him make his first cast off the dock. He started reeling the line back in as I turned around to help one of the other kids rig up. "Grampie, I think I got something," Eric cried out. Sure enough his tiny rod was bent over double and a fish was jumping about some ways out into the river. Eric began reeling as I shouted out instructions. The big fish continued to jump and at first I thought he had hooked into a big sockeye. Eric finally got the fish to the edge of the dock and I netted a beautiful 12 pound rainbow for him. Eric's dad, Chris, used to work for a taxidermist and still had the skills to do a nice mount of my grandson's first trophy fish.

Chapter 18
Rumor Trail Leads to Trophy Pike

Rumors. Whether it be trophy Florida bass, "4 by 4" Kodiak blacktail bucks, "mythical" Dall rams, or "giant" northern pike—these rumors always seem to get my attention. First the rumor, followed by research (to see if there could be any truth to the rumor), then the chase. During these various pursuits I have covered most of the Florida Everglades south of Lake Okeechobee, much of the south end of Kodiak Island, all but one of the major Dall sheep mountain ranges of Alaska, and now nearly a dozen of Alaska's northern pike lakes. Many fish and game based rumors are just that, and often lead to the classical "wild goose chase." I have taken off on many of these rumor-inspired adventures over the years. The latest rumor, which led to my trophy-class pike, started with a secondhand report that went "swear to God, I saw a pike skeleton along the shore of an Iliamna area lake that measured 8-inches across the widest part of the head." As a fisheries biologist (although no pike expert) I was certain that this was an exaggeration. But still, there is usually some element of truth to rumor reports so I felt a little research was in order.

Off to the local Fish and Game office to talk with the sports fish biologists. This led to phone calls to other biologists who are experts on pike and who are responsible for research and management in the Iliamna region. Results of this research were encouraging. Although the largest northern pike in the state are found in tributaries of the Yukon and Kuskokwim rivers, waters of the Iliamna region and out to the west are known to be a close second for pike growth.

On a beautiful mid-March day my son-in- law Chris cranked up the Super Cub in Kenai at 8:15 AM and we were off. We met up with Roy Whitford about halfway across and high in the sky over Cook Inlet and headed to Lake Clark Pass. For safety's sake, these cub pilots like to fly in pairs when headed off on a long range adventure. There was no wind and the mountains loomed sunny and beautiful. Augustine volcano to the south was smoking away. We took a shortcut and passed by just a stone's throw, and just below, the summit of Mount Redoubt. Two hours from takeoff we were into the Iliamna country and decided on one of several known pike lakes in the region to try our luck. Any one of these lakes could produce good-sized pike based on Fish and Game reports. After a smooth landing we drilled a few test holes (yah, I should have brought my portable depth sounder)! These were too shallow with only a foot of water under the ice. We taxied off a short way and tried another spot with the same results. We tried again farther down the lake and this time we found the depth we were looking for.

Chris drilled a couple holes for Roy and me and then headed off about 30 yards to drill one for himself. Roy and I had no sooner got our tip-ups set up and our baits in the water when Chris yelled out, "I got one already!" For the next 90 minutes it was non stop action for all of us with pike up to 29 inches. By this time we had shed our coats and we were actually looking forward to a letup in the action so we could squeeze in a lunch break! We finally got this reprieve and instead of a flag every two or three minutes, it was now down to ten minutes or so.

After lunch the action slowed a little more, but then my flag went up about 25 yards from where I had started to rig some different gear to try. By the time I sloshed through the snow and reached the hole, the line was near the end of the spool. The pike stopped just as I reached the hole, evidently to munch on his herring lunch. I set the hook and at first thought I was hung on the bottom. Then it moved, luckily toward me, since I was short on line. After gathering in a few yards she (most big pike are females) changed directions and the fun began. The line ran speedily through my gloved hands, and then went slack. Here she came toward me again as I gathered in the black Polar line. When she turned and ran again I felt the full weight and realized I had hooked a lunker. My main thought was how I was going to get this fish up through an 8-inch hole in the ice. I was regretting that we hadn't used a 10-inch auger. After two more long runs I got her up to the edge of the hole. By this time Chris and Roy had wandered over to join me to see if I was just B.S.-ing, or if I was really on to something big. Earlier I had experienced some problems in getting a smaller 29 inch pike up through my hole, so they were at first skeptical.

The first two attempts to bring the pike up through the hole didn't work out, since I couldn't get her head turned. On the next try she started to get stuck and the momentum to bring her through the ice was lost. I let the pike run back out again and then tried pulling as fast as I could to gain enough momentum to burst her up through the hole. And that's exactly how she came up—with a burst into the air and out onto the ice! I don't know what the world record is for repeating the phrase "Oh my God, that's a big fish," but I believe Chris now holds it for a real life situation.

We fished for another hour or so and took our pictures. A few more smaller pike were landed and then it was time to head home. We had landed 30 pike and retained 11 in less than four hours of fishing. We had missed another 10-to-12 fish in all. Our pike probably averaged 4-to-5 pounds in weight and along with the monster, we had two 29 inchers that weighed between 7-and-8 pounds.

Lucky on the ice! This 24 pound northern pike barely fit through an 8 inch hole in the ice. Somewhere in Iliamna country. March, 2004.

After landing back in Kenai I stopped at Trustworthy Hardware, where the pike weighed in at 24.6 pounds. A neighbor nearby had a certified scale, where it checked out at 24.3 pounds. The next day I brought the pike to the

137

Soldotna Fish and Game office for trophy certification. They weighed it in at 24-pounds even and recorded an official total length of 46 inches. The sport fish biologist took scale samples which were to be read later, but guessed the pike was about 20 years old. Dave Cozzini, owner of Ninilchik Fish Mounts, stopped by to pick up the pike later that day and said, "I'm from pike country, but this is the largest northern I've ever seen!" He's looking forward to doing a skin mount for me.

Now, I'm enough of a realist to know that I was very lucky and that this was more than likely the biggest pike I'll ever catch. However, I heard a rumor that northerns will get up to 55 inches and more than 40 pounds up along the Yukon River! Perhaps another retirement project.

Chapter 19
Hoot of a Time on the Ho Ho

My neighbor, Ralph Meloon, gave me a call one day in late June, 1994 and invited me on a flight to his lodge on the Holitna River. Since we were between king runs on the Kenai and since I had been hearing Ralph's wild and crazy fish stories about this river in western Alaska, I readily accepted. We left from Longmere Lake in Soldotna in Ralph's 185 floatplane and landed on the Holitna River one hour and forty-five minutes later. As we got out of the plane and started packing our gear up to the lodge we were attacked by virtual hordes of mosquitoes! And some of these were the biggest mosquitoes I'd ever encountered. Not to worry, said Ralph, "We'll don the full-body mosquito suits and they won't bother us too much."

Tarpon of the North

The next morning we set out early as we were going after three different species of fish. First on Ralph's schedule were sheefish, which I had never caught or even seen before. Sheefish, also known as inconnu, are a member of the whitefish family and are only found in arctic and subarctic regions. We headed down river a ways in a small river boat and dropped anchor at the top of a hole at a bend in the river. The hole was quite deep, but sheefish when feeding are pretty much at the surface. This morning they appeared to be feeding actively, perhaps wolfing down migrating salmon fry. We cast our lures into the hole and immediately we both hooked up. I was impressed with the fight as we both hauled in fish in the 10-to-12 pound class. "Oh, these are the small ones," Ralph said. We fished for another hour or so landing several more and then all of a sudden the bite was off. I kept the largest one that I caught, about a 20 pounder, intending to have it mounted later on. Ralph kept a smaller one for the dinner table, which he told me later smelled like fresh cut watermelon. "Well, we did pretty good," Ralph exclaimed, "but in the past we've caught them up to 34 pounds!"

Northern Pike

Now it was time to try our luck at pike fishing and we headed back upstream and pulled off into a side slough of the main river. Pixies and daredevils seemed to be the ticket here and it was not long before we were both hooked up on what I thought were decent-sized fish. After landing a few 25-to-30 inch pike, Ralph informed me that we might have to move to another area to find some bigger ones. So we tried another slough and this time we caught pike three feet long, probably weighing 15 pounds or more. "Oh, these are pretty small too," Ralph smugly relates. We tried another spot but 36 inches was our biggest fish that day. According to Ralph, the pike in this river system get up to 50 inches and more than 35 pounds!

King Salmon, Too

Ralph wanted to now show me some king salmon fishing so we took off upriver to the Hoholitna River, a tributary to the Holitna and about four miles above the lodge. We entered the Ho Ho, and motored upstream for about two miles. So far this day we had seen eagles, ospreys, and moose and as we rounded a bend in the river we added black bear to our wildlife list. The mosquitoes were fierce, but the full-body protective suits did their job well. I have to really wonder how people survived in this region in the days before mosquito repellent and netting became available.

We arrived at Ralph's king salmon fishing hole and began to make a few casts. The run was past its peak and most of the fish had taken on a reddish hue as they approached spawning time. We caught some smaller kings in the 15-to-25 pound class and again Ralph assured me that there are bigger ones to be had. We drifted down river a ways and I hooked into one that put a significant bend into my fishing rod. The big king headed down river and we followed closely in pursuit. This was really fun on the lightweight gear we were using. Finally the fish tired and stopped in a deep hole. Try as I might I couldn't move him out. Looking down into the hole, Ralph could see the fish wrapped around a big log. It was down too deep to net so we poked at him with an oar and eventually ended up breaking him off. We weren't going to keep the king, which we estimated to about 40 pounds, so it was no big loss. We headed back down to the lodge to BBQ up some moose steaks. It had been one heck of a day of fishing and one *Hoot of a Time on the Ho Ho*!

Chapter 20
From the Moon to the Kenai

Most guides who have worked on the Kenai for a number of years at some point get an opportunity to take a celebrity out fishing considering that the Kenai River is known as "world famous!" I have been privileged to take out a few professional athletes and other celebrities but none perhaps as special as an astronaut who actually walked on the surface of the moon. After all, there are only twelve people in the world today who can lay claim to that feat.

When my friend and fellow fishing guide Jim Stogsdill asked me to help out with a party of astronauts who were coming to Kenai for a ground breaking ceremonial for the Challenger Learning Center, I jumped at the chance. As part of their whirlwind tour of the Kenai Peninsula, the astronauts were to have a half-day of silver salmon fishing in the lower Kenai River. About midday of our scheduled trip, Jim and I got word that their tour was running late and that the fishing trip would have to be cut short. As we patiently waited at the Pillars boat landing we received occasional updates on their progress. First we were told the trip would have to be reduced to 3-hours (still not too bad for a silver trip and both Jim and I thought we could put them into some fish); then we were told they would probably only have 2-hours and we started to become a little concerned. When our party of astronauts and their wives finally showed up at the dock we were told by their tour guide "You have to have them back here in one hour because they are scheduled for a gala dinner event at 6 PM." "Thanks a lot, Jack!," I thought, maybe out loud.

I quickly loaded up astronauts Charles "Pete" Conrad Jr., Norman Thagard, and Norman's wife, Kirby, in my boat while Jim loaded up astronauts Walt Cunningham and Alan Bean in his boat. Pete Conrad was the commander of the Apollo 12 mission; America's second manned lunar landing. He was also the third person to ever set foot on the surface of the moon. Norm Thagard had the distinction of five space shuttle missions and was the first American to be assigned to the Mir Space Station. At one time he held the record for longest time in space—3360 hours.

It was an even numbered year and Jim and I thought the best we could do in one hour probably was put them into the more numerous pink salmon, which were near the peak of their run. We motored down toward Eagle Rock and looked for what is the most critical part of a Kenai River silver trip—a good place to anchor. There were many boats out this evening and it didn't look too promising to find a "parking place." But then, as I approached the rock, we lucked out. A guide boat was pulling out of one of the prime locations on the north bank just above the rock. Perhaps he had just limited out and was heading in for the day. I had to be an optimist at this point, now with less than one hour remaining to try and impress someone who has been to, and walked on, the moon!

From the moon to the Kenai. L. to R: Astronaut Norm Thagard, his wife Kirby, guide Loren Flagg, and Astronaut Charles "Pete" Conrad. Just one hour to fish, but we got lucky with a couple silvers in the "teens." Photo by Jerry Poole

I quickly pulled into this prime location and dropped the anchor. It was pretty fast water here, the anchor didn't hold, and we rapidly drifted down toward the boat anchored below us. How embarrassing was this! Commander Pete Conrad, the second man to land a craft on the moon, was able to dock on his first try and here I was unable to dock a small boat along the bank of the river in his presence! Sensing my predicament, Pete, being the natural born leader that he was, immediately sprang into action. Before I could even ask for help he was up in the bow pulling away at the anchor while I slowly taxied forward with the motor. I was impressed and even more when he said "Let's try that again and this time just let *me* know when to drop the hook."

We were now securely anchored up with the lines baited and tossed out. The inside line got snagged on a branch and while I messed with it Pete hooked onto a decent fish. Maybe too decent since the line went screaming off the reel! I usually try to work a fish back to the boat, but in a strong current with a big fish it is often necessary to "release" from the anchor and drift down river with the fish. Since Pete's fish by this time was now about to get wrapped around Eagle Rock, I quickly threw the buoy—which was connected by line to the anchor—off the bow of the boat. We drifted down past Eagle Rock as Pete skillfully brought the big silver back to the boat. I don't think I'd ever been so nervous netting a silver, but managed this task to Pete's compliment of "*good job, skipper!*"

After motoring back to our anchor spot, we now had about 20 minutes left to fish. Norm hooked one, fought it for a bit, and then lost it. Norm's wife, Kirby, then hooked up and we landed another beauty. It was now time to go back to the dock where the two fish together weighed in at 25 pounds. Landing two big silvers like this in the short amount of time we had involved a lot of luck, and I couldn't have asked for more! I was saddened a couple of years later to learn that Commander Pete Conrad had been killed in a motorcycle accident in California.

Epilogue

Many go fishing all their lives without knowing
it is not fish they are after. (Henry David Thoreau)

After more than 55 years of being involved with fish and various types of fisheries I can honestly say, with apologies to Zane Grey, that I have been lucky to be able to blend avocation and vocation. I am happy to say that I have not yet tired of this activity and still remain involved, although now mostly in the sport fishery. Yes, there are times when I despair over the sad state of certain fisheries—for example, the Kenai River king salmon sport fishery. Yet, there is a lot to be thankful for—especially in Alaska, where fisheries management overall has been excellent, the habitat has mostly been adequately maintained, and the salmon returns are in many cases at all-time highs.

The Kenai River

Participation in marine commercial salmon fisheries has been limited for more than 30 years, yet the commercial guide industry has yet to have limits imposed on their numbers. This segment of the fishery has been out of control for sometime now on the Kenai River. Most local residents believe that it is ludicrous to allow more than 300 guides to fish on just one river! The emphasis of the guide industry has focused on a *quantity* fishery as opposed to a *quality* fishery. For many local anglers the Kenai is no longer fun to fish, in fact, has become quite an intimidating experience. As a result, many long-time resident fishermen have become displaced and report that they can no longer stand to be on the river, especially in July. Studies of the river's carrying capacity have borne this out. And now, with the level of total fishing boats reaching more than 600 on certain days in July, hydrocarbon pollution has become an issue.

For too long a time the voice of the resident non-guided angler has not been represented well at Board of Fisheries, and other meetings, where the important decisions are made regarding the Kenai River and other fisheries. Recently, a new group called the Kenai Area Fishermen's Coalition has been formed and is attempting to fill that void. KAFC does not advocate for any commercial interest and their board is composed largely of retired fisheries biologists from state and federal agencies and longtime resident sport fishermen who share a concern for biologically-based management as well as habitat protection. I am a member of this group and I am optimistic that a difference can be made in the long run, and that the Kenai River sport fishery can be returned to a quality experience.

Board of Fish

I have attended many Alaska Board of Fish meetings over the years since 1968. Up until the mid-1990s I felt that the BOF did a good job of weighing the biological information presented to them before making a decision. All this changed in the mid-'90s when the BOF became highly politicized under Governor Tony Knowles' administration. Relevant biological data presented by ADF&G biologists was completely ignored for the first time that I can recall under the new board, which contained Knowles' appointees with an axe to grind against commercial fishermen and a preconceived agenda to follow. The board even refused to allow certain critical reports to be presented when they suspected that the information ran against the grain of their already established positions. Some of the reports shelved by the BOF had to do with environmental and habitat issues within the Kenai River system.

Poor decisions by this board ended up harming the Kenai system and its users for nearly a dozen years before newly appointed board members were able to revisit these decisions and eventually turn things around. There is a fine balance in the Board of Fish process and the injection of politics into decision making invariably destroys this balance. Alaska can hopefully retain its' long established, and highly successful system of biologically based resource management, well into the future.

Cook Inlet Oil Industry

Concerning the oil industry operating in the Cook Inlet Area—there has been significant improvement in the areas of oil spill prevention and response capability in recent years. Most of the progress in this area came post-*Exxon Valdez*. On the federal level it took the Oil Pollution Act of 1990 to bring about major change while on the state level the vehicle for change was House Bill 567, passed by the Alaska Legislature in 1990. This bill strengthened the state's oil pollution control laws and mandated new response planning standards and discharge prevention requirements for offshore facilities and pipelines. I had a part in writing the section of this bill that dealt with Cook Inlet and ended up n Juneau during the final days of the legislative session to lobby and help ensure its passage.

While Cook Inlet may be at less risk from industry related pollution today, than prior to 1990, the risks are still considered by many to be high. Much could be done to improve the safety of operations in the area including implementing the recommendations of the Alaska Oil Spill Commission and the Safety of Navigation report commissioned by the Cook Inlet Regional Citizen's Advisory Council. These include the use of tanker escorts by tractor tugs and the establishment of a Cook Inlet vessel traffic system.

Future Plans

Although my wife, Sandra, and I are both retired from any professional or business connection to the fisheries, we are still involved as sports and personal use fishermen, and also, through association with family members who participate in commercial fisheries. My daughter, Laurie, and her husband, Chris, own a 37-foot drift boat, the *Excalibur*, and participate in the Cook Inlet drift gill net fishery. My son, Mitch, has owned a set net site in past years at Clam Gulch and has also worked for many years as a deck hand in the salmon and herring seine fisheries in Cook inlet and other parts of the state. For several years he worked for Beaver Nelson on the *Nuka Point* out of Homer. He is still active in commercial fishing and this past year worked in the Togiak herring fishery with skipper Rob Nelson on the *Sea Prince*.

Sandra and I plan to stay active in fishing for as long as our health permits. On the Kenai River, we'll select our times carefully and try to avoid periods when crowding is at its worse. For halibut, we'll continue to be "'fair weather" fishermen, and we'll likely be found out on Cook Inlet when the tides are small and the wind is down. We have enjoyed some wonderful fishing on our winter vacations to warmer climes. On our trips to Hawaii we have yet to hook up with a marlin, but have had success with Mahi Mahi and Ono. It took a trip to Cabo San Lucas on the Baja Peninsula of Mexico to catch our first marlin. My old haunts in Florida are where we have headed whenever I get the itch to fish for largemouth bass again. Our future plans include more of these out-of-state-trips as long as the budget and our health hold up. In Alaska the "Spawn 'till you Die" bumper stickers are pretty popular. But, if you see an "Ol' Geezer" running around with a "Fish 'till you Die" bumper sticker, please wave, it could be me!

Fish 'Till You Die

(above left) Retirement Projects: Sandra and I with a pair of bright saltwater kings from Cook Inlet off Stariski Creek. More of this in future plans! Photo by Mitch Flagg

(above right) I caught this 30 pound Ono while fishing with Captain Sam Miller off the "Big Island" of Hawaii in the mid-1980s. Excellent eating fish!

(left) Sandra caught this nice Mahi Mahi on the same trip fishing with Sam Miller off the Kona Coast.

(above left) We tried in Hawaii but it took a trip to Cabo San Lucas, Mexico to score on our first marlin. These "stripers" weighed in at 90 (L.) and 100 pounds. February, 1988.

(above right) Retirement also means having time to take friends fishing on the Kenai. We'll pick our times carefully! Pat Dwinnell with an early run king from Big Eddy, June, 2007.

(below) Residents may harvest salmon with dip nets. Lee Kempf and Russell Dukowitz display their first sockeye of the season on the 4th of July. Kasilof River mouth, 2004.

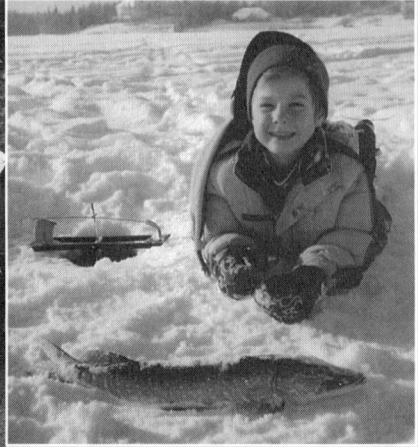

(above) Retirement means having a little more time to take the grandsons fishing, winter or summer. Eric Kempf with a pike taken at Scout Lake.

(above) Retirement also means having the time to visit relatives and friends around the country. Daughter Laurie and I are ready to feast on lobsters at a family reunion and New England style clambake in Friendship, Maine. August, 2006.

(right) L. to R: Sandra's sister, Paula Leavenworth, Russell Dukowitz, and Sue Dukowitz display three nice silver salmon from the Kenai River.

150

Sources

Alaska Department of Fish and Game. Environmental Studies of Kachemak Bay and Lower Cook Inlet. Volume 1. 1977. Impact of Oil on the Kachemak Bay Environment. Anchorage, Alaska.

Alaska Department of Fish and Game. Recommendations and Biological Justification for the "Buy Back" of Leases within the 28th Oil and Gas Lease Sale in Kachemak Bay. 1977. Anchorage, Alaska.

Alaska Magazine. Kachemak Bay-Richest in the World? Article by Loren Flagg. February, 1975. Alaska Northwest Publishing. Anchorage, Alaska.

Alaska Oil Spill Commission. 1990. SPILL-The Wreck of the *Exxon Valdez.* Implications for Safe Transportation of Oil. Anchorage, Alaska.

Alaska Seas and Coasts. Volume 2, Number 5. 1974. Oil in Kachemak Bay. University of Alaska Sea Grant Program. Anchorage, Alaska.

Anchorage Daily News. Various published articles. 1973-1977. Anchorage, Alaska.

Anchorage Times. Various published articles. 1973-1977. Anchorage, Alaska.

Davidson, Art. 1990. *In the Wake of the Exxon Valdez.* Sierra Club Books. San Francisco, California.

Dineen, J. Walter. 1965-1966. Everglades Impoundment Fisheries Investigation. Annual Progress Report for D.J. Project F-16-R-4. Florida Game and Fresh Water Fish Commission. Tallahassee, Florida.

Douglas, Marjory Stoneman. 1997. 50th Anniversary Edition. *The Everglades River of Grass.* Pineapple Press Inc. Sarasota, Florida.

Flagg, Loren B. 1976. Testimony before Alaska House Resources Committee on H. B. 626 Relating to Establishment of Marine Sanctuaries and Condemnation of the Kachemak Bay Oil and Gas Leases. ADF&G, Homer, Alaska.

Flagg, Loren B. 1992. Cook Inlet, Alaska: A 30 Year History of Commercial Fishing and Oil Industries Operating Concurrently in an Offshore Subartic Environment. Presentation to 2nd International Conference on Fisheries and Offshore Petroleum Exploitation. Bergen, Norway.

Flagg, Loren B. 1963-2007. Daily Activities Log—Fisheries Issues. Kenai, Alaska.

Homer News. Various published articles. 1973-1977; 1989. Homer, Alaska.

Kizzia, Tom. 1978. *How Fishermen Kept the Oil Industry out of Kachemak Bay.* Alaska Fisherman. Juneau, Alaska.

Panitch, Mark. 1975. Offshore Drilling: Fishermen and Oilmen Clash in Alaska. *Science Magazine,* Volume 189, No. 4198. Washington, D.C.

About the Author

Loren Flagg grew up in Massachusetts where he graduated from East Bridgewater High School and later the University of Massachusetts at Amherst where he received a Bachelor of Science degree in wildlife biology. After graduation from college he worked as a fisheries biologist for the states of Massachusetts and Florida before moving with his family to Alaska in 1968.

Living in Homer, Loren worked for the Alaska Department of Fish and Game as a commercial fisheries management biologist and later as a habitat biologist assigned to the Kachemak Bay marine research project. In this capacity he played a key role in the state's repurchase of the Kachemak Bay oil leases during the mid-1970s.

The Flaggs moved to Soldotna in 1979 where Loren then worked for the Fisheries Rehabilitation, Enhancement and Development Division until his retirement from ADF&G in 1987. After retirement from the state he worked as a consultant to the commercial fisheries industry and as a sport fishing guide on the Kenai River. In April 1989 he was hired by the Kenai Peninsula Borough to head up the Cook Inlet area response to the *Exxon Valdez* oil spill. Following the oil spill he served on the congress established Cook Inlet Regional Citizen's Advisory Council as a member of the Prevention, Response, and Operations committee. He also served on the Kenai River Special Man-

agement Area Advisory Board in the early 1990s.

Loren and his wife, Sandra, now live in Kenai, Alaska where the municipal golf course serves as their back yard and Cook Inlet and the Kenai River are nearby.

Index